The Armchair Millionaire

Building Wealth With
Real Estate Investments

Jason Meier

ISBN: 978-1-77277-122-0

Published by
10-10-10 Publishing
Markham, Ontario
CANADA

Contents

Foreword

Jason Meier is based in Canada and completed his first house flip 11 years ago. This is where Jason discovered his passion for real estate investing, leading him to create REI Consulting Inc. and now he works in this industry full time. In this book, *The Armchair Millionaire*, Jason explains the ways he can make you above average returns on your investment with his company, even during a recession!

Jason discusses the pros and cons of three ways to make money using real estate as an investment. He initially begins; however, with a discussion of the importance of duplicating yourself (automation) and the utilization of CRM (Customer Relationship Management) software to make the best use of your only limited resource, which is time. The first of the three ways to make money investing in real estate is the "flip." This technique includes buying at a discount, quickly fixing up the building and then selling it for a profit. You also have the option of renting it out to create short-term cash flow and long-term increased property value. Jason then explores possibilities such as rent-to-own scenarios and wholesaling—where the investor takes a house under contract and then sells that right to purchase, at a higher price, to an investor who has the wherewithal to renovate and flip the property.

In his own words, Jason says to you, "The Armchair Millionaire is a detailed program for finding, fixing, selling, or holding onto real estate—in a profit oriented fashion." *The Armchair Millionaire* is filled with such gems, all thoroughly explained within these pages.

This book is a must read to grow your serious interest in real estate investing into financial success. Learn all the great information that Jason has provided for you.

Raymond Aaron
New York Times Bestselling Author, Real Estate Investor

Chapter One

The Introduction

Every so often the most advanced countries in the world have witnessed a decline in their respective economies, followed by a subsequent boom in production. This repeated pattern in business tends to reoccur every 20–30 years and is what's called a business cycle.

A business cycle features a peak and a trough. You can assume that the peak phase of the cycle is characterized by lower unemployment rates, higher income and happy business owners. Also, product prices are higher, which would inconvenience the consumer if their income falls.And that's what happens at the beginning of a recession. As incomes rise, prices follow suit. The population changes as well, forcing companies to increase their output as their demand is on the rise. Through the years, the increase in demand strains companies, causing production to decrease and, with it, incomes. During every recession in a business cycle, many workers are laid off and the unemployment line lengthens.

We're not talking about a depression, which is when the economy decreases to where businesses start to shut down. Such a trough in the business cycle would be comparable to the Great Depression in the United States, where millions of Americans were living in poverty and struggling to find work because of the stock market crash in 1929. The Second World War was able to boost the economy again, since weaponry, supply production and troops were much-needed occupations. Many people began filling these jobs to participate in the war. This led to much economic prosperity during the following decades of the 1950s-1970s.

Since World War II, the United States has undergone at least one minor recession (some of the shortest ones lasted only 6–8 months before transitioning to economic recovery) per decade. The 1990s was a decade with the longest period of economic growth. This lasted up until the terrorist attacks of September 11, 2001. However, as the United States was launched into the War on Terrorism, economic recovery once again took the stage.

The next recession in the United States began in 2007, and the economy thereafter descended to its lowest point in many years by March 2009. But, once banks started receiving government bailout money, the financial outlook for businesses, their employees, and their customers, improved.

Now, the economy in the United States is on the road to recovery. In many states, gas prices have plummeted to below $2 a gallon, showing that the demand has increased, something that will pump more money into the economy, so as long as the oil is available. When the demand increases and supply decreases, that's when the economy could be approaching the danger zone.

My point is that no matter where you live, whether you're in Alberta or Washington, D.C., it is entirely normal for the gross domestic product (GDP) of a country's financial structure to fluctuate over the years. A country can be facing a recession, but, in time, the government will adapt to whatever factors caused the economy to decrease. They do this with the hopes that the economy will take a turn for the better. Often it does just that.

The individual is very much affected by a recession. Let's say he works for a company that has been very prosperous for a while. Then, when the price of a material increases, the company decides that they can no longer afford to keep him, so they let him go. Without the job that once supported this hardworking man, he now has trouble finding a job in an economy where companies are downsizing. For those who still have work, but where companies are desperate to bring their costs down, their wages could be frozen or even cut, causing everyone to have less money.

Therefore, during a business cycle, a nation affected by a recession is negatively impacted. It's hard to tell at the time, but a recession could either turn into a depression, or the economy could recover just as quickly. It depends on governmental policies, population changes, or what's happening on Wall Street.

The housing market is a reflection of how companies are affected in the business cycle. They are part of the real estate industry, which occupies a huge portion of a national GDP. Economic fluctuations dictate government policies, which influence mortgage and interest rates. During the peak phase, when business is booming, more people will be employed. The more people employed, the more money everyone will have. This means housing prices will rise, because it costs more money to construct a home. The only thing decreasing at this time is the unemployment rate. At this point, nearly every citizen is utilized. Consequently, this would mean that mortgage and interest rates are going to be higher than during an economic bust.

At the start of a recession, you'll notice that more and more people are losing their jobs. Because this would create a discrepancy to money coming in versus money going out, many of the unemployed find that they cannot make payments for their homes. Ergo, they lose their homes to the banks—a lengthy, legal process called **foreclosure**. In order to not lose the value of their assets, the bank attempts to sell the repossessed houses at a lower price. These "deals" could look attractive to a potential investor.

So what if I were to tell you, the investor, that in light of a recession you *can* make more money? You can benefit by investing in these two words: **real estate.**

Now at first, you might say, "But Jason, times are hard! I can't afford a house in this ridiculous market."

It's not just about being able to afford a house; this book explains the many ways you can prosper in real estate investments during a recession. Throughout the numerous chapters in this book, I explain to you what real estate investing is all about, the methods to going about investing and how you can benefit from all of this when times are tough. I won't say it will happen overnight, but if you follow the directions in this book and be patient, I will get your money to work for you. All of a sudden, you won't need to worry about whether or not you can afford a house, in any economy!

The Armchair Millionaire discusses how investment works in the 21st century. Investors have been relocating their portfolios to cyberspace as automated investing is becoming more popular. Another strategy you will get to hear about is the rent-to-own option, where you can not only give others a place to live, but by doing this, you can acquire more money! I'll also introduce you to some home improvement, as wholesaling offers renovations to low-value homes, making them good as new, and perfect to sell.

Of course, in this book, I won't ignore the fact that recessions cause foreclosures, resulting in many individuals losing their homes. I'm also going to explain why this happens and how you can regain financial footing if you've had the unfortunate experience of having your house repossessed.

"But Jason, what about stocks? I could do just fine investing in those," you could say. There may be some companies with relatively promising stocks, but everybody needs a place to live, especially if they have been affected with a foreclosed home. Plus, because of the lower mortgage interest rates that occur during a recession, you will be able to invest in real estate with ease.

So here's how the layout of *The Armchair Millionaire* is going to be. I want you to get a good idea of what happens to your money during a recession. In each chapter, I will delve into the many aspects of real estate and how it is affected by a recession. If you're no stranger to investing, bear with me, for I will explain all terms for those who are just getting started with investing. What does it mean to "flip houses?" Does "wholesaling" mean to buy houses in bulk? Throughout the following chapters, I will gladly elaborate, for the goal is for me to direct this book to everyone.

Investing is a smart way to stretch your money and acquire more paychecks. If you're currently frustrated with your financial situation, that's personal, but I cannot stress enough that you can take advantage of buying and selling houses during a recession, which will help people find a place to live, and also make you richer. Allow me to explain how, with my book, *The Armchair Millionaire*.

Chapter Two

"I Am the Recession-Investment-Automator!"

By nature, humans seek convenience in everything they do. Since the invention of the wheel, society's brightest minds have continually developed more sophisticated technology, and we rely on these advancements to make life simpler. Nowadays, snack machines replace concession stands, while Priceline and Orbitz replace travel agents.

To automate something means to make it complete a repetitive function at a certain time—to make it automatic. It does what you want it to do without you having to be there to control what it does. You might program your coffee-maker to start when you wake up at the same time each day. Congratulations, you've just automated the way you make your coffee, buying you time for your morning routine.

And real estate? Well, anyone can begin investing in real estate. You can make an offer on a house, buy it, increase its net worth (this may take some home improvement) and sell it to a person to make a profit. However, if you were to manage several other properties, further on in your career, how would you find the time to take care of it all, especially if you have a full-time job, school and a family? I'm not saying it's impossible. It doesn't even have to be overwhelming. But to start a real estate investing business, you must have a plan and some cash (I'll tell you why later in the chapter).

Also, another thing to bear in mind is to be patient. Successful real estate investing does not happen overnight. At first, you may have a rough time with attracting a lead, or finding a property to put money into. The business cycle doesn't stay in one place, and neither do people. But if you have time and ambition, you will land a deal on a house and go from there.

The best thing about investing is that you don't have to do it all on your own. Real estate investing has gone from just one person juggling all the roles of lawyer, accountant and handyman, to employing the help of experts in money management and legal protection. Having help can make your investment business more efficient and convenient.

In the real estate investment business, there are certified professionals who are properly trained to assist you, the real estate investor/businessperson. They help you with filing income taxes, dispensing legal advice, managing your portfolios, and securing a mortgage on a property. These people are your teammates, helping you navigate the world of the housing market. They might likely require a cut of what you earn in house-selling, but when it comes to the managing of your real estate investment business, they are your confidantes, and your best friends.

Let me introduce to you your team of financial advisors. The first "draft pick" will be your **mortgage broker.** This guy/gal is very much similar to a car salesman, in the sense that he acts as a middleman between the bank (the institution loaning you money) and you, the potential homeowner/investor.

When you meet with a mortgage broker, they assess your income, your employment, and some basic information about who you are as a borrower, which is often generated in the form of a credit report. The broker relays this information to the bank, who is the ultimate decider as to whether or not your mortgage is approved.

Hiring a mortgage broker can save you time. Unlike a loan officer who only works with one bank, a mortgage broker does the shopping for you. They can look at rates from multiple banks and lenders so you don't have to apply for a mortgage multiple times. Instead, he/she has the information you gave them, so you can relax knowing that a fiduciary is handling your affairs with professionalism.

The next person you'll want to see about starting your real estate investment business is a **real estate lawyer.** Investing in legal counsel is necessary to buying or selling property. There are contracts you'll have to sign, and having a lawyer around during the signing will help you interpret the complicated "legalese" some of them will present. Furthermore, you don't want to be bogged down by a deal you cannot escape. Having a real estate lawyer review legal documents for you can save you much-needed time, money, and hassles.

In choosing a real estate lawyer to conduct business with you, choose one who is experienced in real estate law. The more up-to-date they are with the changing laws, the more useful they'll be in informing you of your legal options. Invest in a good one and your business in real estate will thank you.

Never forget that the taxman waits for no one. If you start your real estate investing business one year, the CRA (in Canada) will want to know about it by the next April. Get in good with them by having a skilled **real estate accountant** by your side. This MVP on your investment team keeps track of all of your business transactions on the properties you manage.

They know the ins-and-outs of the legalities on tax codes. Having that knowledge vested in them, they can maximize your profits.

Throughout your investing career, you might purchase some properties that require beautifying. The conditions may be abhorrent at first, so in order to sell the place for a higher value, you'll want to fix it up and make it as if it were new. That's why you want to find a **contractor** who can make repairs and improvements. Look for them at hardware stores by asking the cashiers. Post an advertisement on Craigslist.

A major step in creating an automated business is being wise as to who you want to hire. It's your money that you choose to invest in these people. You get to decide who's most suitable to join you in your investing ventures. Take the time to find the most informed lawyer, skilled accountant, and handiest handyman, all making up your most reliable assets in your real estate business.

In selecting these team players, it is important to know who you're hiring. Conduct interviews if you find multiple candidates equally eligible for your work. In the business conversations you schedule with them, you are questioning their credibility. You must make sure they arrive punctually and are dressed for the part, whether they dress in business casual like an accountant or as a construction worker who is ready, willing, certified and able to operate on your properties.

So, when you conduct interviews, the kind of information you want to find out from your candidates is their education and work experience. You can ask to see samples of their work and talk to their references to grab more insight on who you're working with. Ask about their rates and what fees they charge.

Interviews give a feel for how you might interact with your potential personnel.

The above mentioned tactics are useful for in-house automation. **Outsourcing,** the other method of automation, refers to relaying tasks to people in locations elsewhere, or taking legal and financial aspects to the internet in order to make investors' real estate businesses run more smoothly. These techniques do not require you to conduct interviews or background checks. Nevertheless, it would be wise for you to shop around and find the automation method most suitable to your needs.

Outsourcing is one way to multi-task in your investing, since it allows you to handle several properties at once. If you are interested in a property on the other side of the country, you might want to get a local building contractor to scope the place and gather estimates on costs of repairs/improvements, and subsequently make them. You can hire real estate agents to hold open houses, mail flyers, and post advertisements in local newspapers to get potential occupants of your property interested.

This method of automating your real estate business leaves you with just the tasks of creating purchase offers, touching base with the real estate agents and contractors in your property areas, and deciding as to where else you would want to conduct business.

Using VAs or **virtual assistants** (generally what we call them) has become a growing trend, especially since the world today has become connected by the advancements of technology. To hire a VA means to outsource by relocating your tasks elsewhere. You may have heard of large companies outsourcing jobs to countries like India, where call center agents are most utilized to answer customer service questions.

How hiring VAs pertains to real estate is that you too can relocate your tasks abroad to real estate lawyers, handymen and realtors, negotiating with them for sensible prices. Find properties in the location you desire, within your budget, and put your money where your house is. In turn, all of this will help you capitalize on more properties, making money virtually everywhere!

As your real estate investing campaign expands and gains more leverage, you will learn of ways to outsource. Ask around the community of investors for tactics and techniques to secure properties and potential income from afar. If you are just beginning, consider investing in properties locally to ensure the confidence that your business ventures will be viable elsewhere.

So, now that we've discussed the ways you can utilize people to help efficiently stretch your income by investing in real estate, let's move onto more ways to automate your investing. This is another path you can take in becoming a **Real Estate Investor.**

Developments in 21st century technology have now made it possible to order a pizza with the swipe of a thumb. But you can do much more than just that. Consider **robo-advisors**, online investment assistants that can design a personalized portfolio or an accumulation of all of your investments (expect for yours to grow the more experienced in investing you get).

During the US financial crisis of 2008, robo-advisors were utilized to give investors a more modern feel to managing their assets. Wealth management software makes it easier for clients to access advice and savings plans for college and retirement. It has become user-friendly, asking the investor questions about themselves to design a custom-made investment plan. Some programs like Betterment are more suitable to those just starting out. Others are geared toward the more experienced investor. Nevertheless, robo-advising is a cost-efficient way to manage your finances. Decide for yourself if online automation is the way to go.

Here is some more Economics 101 for you, and, this time, let's talk about how a collapsing economy affects businesses and labor. A recession is the time when many people find themselves laid off due to downsizing. Demand decreases, causing the supply to decrease. Why make more products than people are willing to buy? A surplus amount of product only strains the company's resources, causing the corporation to become less efficient. Product is wasted and money goes down the toilet. With less needed to be made, companies shed excess products and manpower just as a snake sheds its old skin.

So the downside of the recession is that people lose their jobs; putting it bluntly, their employers no longer need their services or just can't afford their services. The laid-off employees must look elsewhere for work. If you are in need of a team to help automate your business, reaching out to Jason and his team should be your first step. They have work experience and are skilled in automation.

Automating your real estate investing during a recession is a smart idea, since it helps create jobs (if you choose to localize your real estate operations). You may be helping someone out who has just lost their job due to corporate drawdowns. As well, you are doing yourself a favor by putting less work on yourself. That helps take off all that stress created by the recession. You don't have to know how to work a chainsaw or know the ins-and-outs of real estate law to invest. You just have to know who to work with and what you're signing up for.

Now that we've gone over what automation is in relation to your real estate investment plan, let's discuss how to automate effectively. There are numerous tasks others can do for you in order to make your real estate investment business successful.

One way to involve the help of other people is to establish your presence on social media. Make a Facebook page for your real estate investment business. These days, almost everyone has a social media account. There are many outlets to choose from, including LinkedIn, Twitter, Facebook, or Instagram. Keep in mind the demographic with whom you want to communicate. Who do you think wants to buy a house the most—an Instagram-addicted twenty-something still in college or a professional businessman with an active LinkedIn account?

No matter which social media platform you choose to use to advertise your properties, remember to keep all of your accounts professional (post nothing you wouldn't want your grandmother to see). Also, regularly keep your followers engaged. Always answer any promising messages they send you, for they could end up being a potential buyer.

Although social media is a great way to automate your real estate marketing, there are some aspects you should regularly carry out yourself.

It is impossible to automate good customer service. Clients who are interested in your houses all have situations unique to them. A simple "Thank you for your interest" email isn't a horrible way to acknowledge inquiries, but it doesn't answer as to when the house was built or the time it was last renovated. In becoming a reliable investor, you should invest time in addressing clients and helping provide them information about their questions. This will help establish credibility, because, in the eyes of potential buyers, being able to get accurate information about the house they want means you're more trustworthy to them.

Once you accrue more interested clients, you can start what's called **Customer Relationship Management,** or a CRM. This is a database that helps you keep track of all your properties and contact information of the customers interested in them. Over months of motivated investing and busywork, it can be a little tough keeping track of all those pesky papers. Some investors might try to organize their data using Microsoft Excel, but the more experience they acquire in the real estate game, the harder it is to account for their spreadsheets, as numerous properties and clients fill up their columns. Luckily, we have been created and tailored a CRM for investors who just want a program to input all of their data. Using a CRM helps the investor grab easy access to everything they want to know about their multiple properties and is one way to make real estate investment automating simpler.

You can modify your CRM however you desire. Online, you may search for CRM programs that appeal the most to you, but beware—some programs lack the ability sync other great systems with it, while others do; you purchase our real estate investor CRM at www.InvestorSolutions.ca.

Real estate investing is challenging and time-consuming. It involves many roles that you may not be able to fill. This requires the help of additional people who will help guide you through the legal and financial parameters of buying and selling homes. Automation, in reference to real estate investing, will take the unnecessary stress off of managing multiple properties, if done right.

To help you get started, you must do some searching for a reliable team of mortgage brokers, real estate lawyers, accountants, and contractors. Ask around for people who have had years of experience in the real estate industry and are knowledgeable in the job they do.

You can decide to automate your real estate business by hiring a handyman to maintain the property in order for it to appeal to potential buyers. Get in contact with a real estate agent to post signs and do some of the advertising for you. They can sit down with you to discuss marketing strategies and contacting leads. These are just some examples of the help you have out there as you consider methods of getting your real estate investing off the ground.

Another way of automating is by taking things to the internet. Using various social media platforms like Facebook and LinkedIn can help increase your exposure, especially among younger audiences who want to buy their first house. Use this to your advantage by sharing advertisements on your profile or your business's Facebook page, and you will rake in more interested buyers than initially imagined.

You can use computers to help in automating your real estate investing business. There are countless programs that organize client contact and property information. Never has it been more easier to access all data in one place, where you will not make the mistake of losing information (unless, of course, your computer crashes, in which case you will have to remember to save all your data regularly).

In a recession, it is a smart idea to decide to use automation. Your need for other people to help you regulate your business can add to the economy by providing a new job for those who may have recently lost one. By relocating your tasks to a region where perhaps the economy is not as bad, you can use this difference to your advantage by being able to pay less for the services you need.

If you use the information in this chapter to apply to your real estate investing, and do it wisely, you can proudly call yourself the "Recession-Investment-Automator!"

Chapter Three

Flipping to Success

Now that we covered the basics of real estate, the economy, and the "Most Valuable Players" on your real estate investing team, let's get *down and dirty* with respect to acquiring and selling houses.

There are many tactics for selling properties that will generate terrific revenue. You might even have seen some TV shows about investors fixing up run-down, 80-year-old bungalows to look good-as-new and ready to sell to happy-go-lucky yuppie couples. It's not going to be as easy as that. You see, unlike what these characters on the home improvement shows make real estate out to be, much work is required on your end to effectively flip houses for ready-to-sell success. House flipping is a commitment, for many reasons. Don't treat it as a hobby, as buying another house is one investment that can affect your financial future. If you take this real estate investment tactic seriously, you will benefit greatly and become savvy about house flipping.

Flipping entails buying a low-value house for the purpose of renovating it and reselling it for a higher profit. This involves getting your hands dirty (literally) and networking, both of which may seem daunting at first, but once you flip a few houses you'll become accustomed to the hard work real estate investing entails.

Before you start flipping houses, there is much to determine. First of all, if you're married and have a family, determine as to whether or not your spouse is on board with your investment plans. The whole process will be that much easier if they are willing to join you by helping with the essential duties.

There is a myriad of information out there for eager investors like you, so conduct some research in all aspects of house flipping. Look at the housing market in your neck of the woods: How much are houses selling for, and how long are they staying on the market? You might be able to get this information from a real estate agent or a friend who possesses knowledge of the housing economy where you live. Also, be aware that you don't have to look for flipping opportunities only where you live. Just make sure you research ahead of time in the areas where you want to flip. This gives you the advantage of knowing whether or not those areas are worth investing in before you spend any money.

In a recession, this may be the best technique for you to use. People lose their jobs more often. So, in order to save money, they'll tend to relocate to cheaper housing, such as apartments, to conserve money. Those who cannot keep up with their mortgage payments end up defaulting on their loans, which forecloses their property. Consequently, in Canada, banks sell these houses for fair market value. To you, the real estate investor, this is a waste of time. You want to market to people who are struggling to pay their bills and offer to purchase the home before the banks foreclose. You want to offer below market value so you can fix them up, generating big profits for you!

However, do be aware that buying a Pre-foreclosure house, normally needs to happen quickly as the homeowner may lose the house to foreclosure at any time. This is dependent upon how long it's been since the home owner stopped paying the mortgage to the bank, the general timeframe being from 4 – 6 months from the time they stopped paying their mortgage. This is because banks, must file legal paperwork against the incumbent tenant.

Here are four simple steps to flipping your first house:

1. Buying. At this stage, you determine everything. What region are you focusing on? Would you like to focus on properties in rural British Columbia, or somewhere in the tropics? And then, consider the kind of house you want to flip. Will it have two bedrooms or four? Think about how much money you have to spend and how much work you can put into the house you wish to buy. This will establish your inventory.

An inventory of successful house flippers includes properties in areas people want to live in. Nobody wants to live in an area with high crime rates. A house near a school, a supermarket, or a hospital, for example, is more likely to sell than a house in a slummy neighborhood. Heck, if you really want a challenging flip, look on the streets for a house needing the most work. With time and dedication, you can flip this inhabitable humble abode into a house that is actually livable.

In the real estate investing industry, one way to find the best houses to flip is called "driving for dollars." This is where you drive around and find houses that will sell for dollars. Find vacant houses, especially those that are in bad shape. You'll know when you see one, when you pass by a house with overgrown grass, an accumulation of weeds or boarded-up windows. At first, this may be unsightly, but for house flipping such properties posses plenty of potential. Keep a notebook and a camera ready so when you return home you can review your notes and pictures to determine what to do with each place. As you narrow down your list of options, drive by the houses that caught your attention and see if they remain vacant for a while, or if any work has been applied to the house. If you decide you want to pursue a specific house from this search, look up the address of the property and the residents that live there. You might be able to find this information at your city hall. If you can successfully reach the incumbent owner of that property, request information from them about the place. What does it look like on the inside? How long has it been vacant? And how much would they offer it to you for, *as is*?

Trust your instinct when setting budgets and looking at deals. If the offer seems too good to be true, then it most likely is. Visit the property in person before determining whether or not papers get signed. Emotions have a way of clouding judgment to a point where a person ends up getting himself in hot water without even realizing it. Don't let your excitement for flipping houses get to where you make a decision that could jeopardize your flip.

One important factor to consider when creating your house inventory is what the *after repair value* (ARV) of each house is going to look like. You add value to a property by fixing it up, if needed. Such expenses add up. So, your goal is to try to buy a house below the current fair market value and tally up the expenses for the flip, including the profit margin you want to make, and then sell the house for the ARV to make your profit. After you determine the ARV, you will know how much to sell the house for.

It is also up to you to determine if, in the near future, the house will appreciate or depreciate in value. Let's suppose that you have a choice of two houses to flip. One is a quaint little cottage that was built during the first half of the 20th century, and the other is a split-level built in 2005. Both are the same price. The first house may seem promising with its antique architecture, but if the foundation is unstable due to its age, it'll lose money very quickly because of the amount of upkeep spent on maintenance. You're better off going with the house built in 2005, since the house will most likely require less work. Consequently, this house is more likely to appreciate in value.

Here is how you should determine the purchase price of a house flip …

Suppose houses in the area where you're interested in flipping are going for $200,000 all fixed up. This will be your ARV. So, you begin with $200,000 then you work your numbers backwards. You market in that area and find an owner who wants to move out of a house that needs some repairs. Let's say they are willing to take $135,000 for the house. You then need to get an estimate for the repairs that are needed to bring the home up to the $200,000 ARV. The estimate comes in at $23,000 for the repairs to the home. You will now need to start calculating the rest of the expenses like the mortgage payments, insurance, taxes, utilities and your profit margin for the project. Based on the $135,000 purchase price the owner is asking for, the mortgage payment would be $631/month @ 5% interest and 20% down payment. The taxes are $100/month and the insurance is $100/month. Talk with the contractor to get a realistic time frame to have the repairs to the home completed—in this case let's say two months. Then you have to list the home for sale and you should budget that it may sit there for three-four months as you are selling at the top of the market in that area. Also, during the renovation and the time the home is listed for sale you will also need to pay all the utilities. In this case let's say that would be $250/month.

Now that you have all the information you need, you can begin to calculate this deal. All the monthly expenses tally up to $1081/month. You need to have $23,000 for the repairs, but it's smart to have at least 10-15% more for unexpected things that are discovered while renovating. So, the renovation budget is $26,450. Six months was planned for this flip at $1,081/month, which equals $6,486. Then you need to budget legal costs for purchasing and selling the home ($1000 for the purchase and then $1800 for the sale is what we will use in this example). You want to be able to make $20,000 profit on this six month flip so you add that as well. When you sell the home the realtor needs to get paid as well, He gets paid 4% of the sold property value, which will be $8,000 based on the $200,000 selling price. That's it; you've got everything you need.

To figure out what you need to purchase the house for, calculate $200,000 less mortgage payments, insurance, taxes for six months, realtor, renovation costs, utilities, legal costs and profit.

$200,000
- mortgage payments for six months = $3,786
- Insurance payments for six months = $600
- Taxes for six months = $600
- Renovation costs with buffer = $26,450
- Legal costs = $2,800
- Utilities for six months = $1,500
- Realtor costs = $8,000
- Profit = $20,000

Total = $136,264

Thus, your purchase price needs to be at or below $136,264. As you can see if you accepted the purchase price the owner wanted of $135,000 you would have an extra $1,264 to use or add to your final profit margin.

Take some time to really analyze your flip before committing to anything. Knowing the ARV is the first part in beginning your flip analysis. An ARV, along with a timeline, mapping out all of the steps and a date intended to sell, makes a big difference in the amount of money you'll earn in the end. Don't let your house be on the market longer than you want it to be. You get to decide ahead of time; create a target date for when you want to see the house sold and stick with that for the duration of the flip. This means you don't get to be sloppy and change the *sell-by* date in the middle of the project to buy yourself some time. And for this reason, I cannot stress enough that a house flip must be well-planned ahead.

2. Financing. The next step in house flipping is determining how you're going to invest in your project. If you do not have the capital in your pockets to pay for one whole house, you can finance your house by going to a bank that is willing to set you up with a mortgage, or a home loan. Otherwise, another technique is to initiate a joint venture (JV), where a second party steps in and contributes to financing your house. The project is still in your hands; you decide which house to buy and how to sell it, but the other person who backed you up will keep 50% of the profit you make by selling the house. There are numerous ways for anybody to be financially equipped to begin flipping houses for profit, but one thing to know is how to pay for it. You don't want to be scrambling around for money halfway through the project with no way out.

Banks consider house flips as high-risk projects, so sometimes they may not be willing to give you a loan. Other times, they won't finance homes that aren't finished. If you have difficulty obtaining a mortgage through a bank, consider going to a hard money lender. These companies are comprised of corporate or individual lenders who provide short-term loans, holding the house as collateral. Since hard money lenders do not require the traditional credit standards to be able to give you a loan, they generally hike up the interest rates to protect from defaulting. That is, these loans are more expensive than regular mortgages. Therefore, use a hard money lender if you find yourself backed into a corner. Don't avoid them completely, but then again, consider this option as m ore of a last resort.

Sit down and figure out your budget, allocating money to different areas of the house where work is needed. At this point, you don't have to shop around for quotes, but now is the time to set parameters for how much you want to spend on each service. If you think fixing water pipes is going to cost up to $,1000 or $2,000, plan to set aside $2,000 for the pipes. Estimating higher will allow you a safety cushion, in case pipe repairs come out to be $1,500. You have some flexibility in your spending, yet you have a limit as to how much you can spend on each facet of preparing the house to sell.

3. Home Improvement. The next fundamental in house flipping is fixing it up. This process is called rehabbing. As I said earlier in the chapter, you can find a dusty old house that sells for cheap and make repairs to it, increasing its market value. Look for potential in houses needing rehabbing and know what repairs will be needed. Since the ARV becomes higher with more work done to the property, you can now sell the house for more than what you paid for, generating a profit. But be careful that the cost of labor and repairs don't exceed the initial value of the house. This is something that is up to you to determine. Once you have acquired a house, make a list of repairs that you want to make to the house and collect a few quotes from potential contractors. This way, you're providing yourself with a choice as to how much you wish to spend. Time, patience, and planning are all of the essence when it comes to a house flip needing extensive rehabbing.

The top four faults in a house that must be tended to immediately have to do with issues in the foundation, roof, plumbing, and electrical systems. Do what it takes to make sure these areas meet federal regulations, as well as local safety ordinances.

Keep the buyers in mind when making renovations to the house. You might want to paint all the walls a loud magenta, but what if an otherwise interested customer doesn't like the color pink? Keep the walls a conservative white or tan to appeal to all potential tenants. Create a house that most people would want, so more people can imagine themselves living there. And pay attention to the other houses in the neighborhood as well. Just because granite countertops would look good in your house, doesn't mean they would also coordinate with the other houses around yours.

In this stage of the flip, it would be a good idea to possess some knowledge about home improvement. There could be some repairs you can learn how to do by yourself. The more you're able to fix, the more money you're saving by not having to hand the job over to somebody else. The only tasks I would highly recommend hiring a contractor for are the tasks that involve heavy equipment or hazardous materials. Improper training about these components may lead to serious injury, and even death.

When looking for a contractor to operate on your house, don't hire any close friends or family. Things happen, and the process of house flipping can be too stressful. Risking losing money is one thing, but you don't want to lose friends over a misunderstanding. This is one reason to keep negative emotions separate from house flipping. Think of this all as a positive money-making experience.

Finding the right contractor can take a little bit of time, as they must be booked well in advance, and some of them might not have the qualifications to carry out some of the work needed on the house. Once you set yourself up with a handyman, ensure that they understand exactly what you want done to the house. The best contractors are licensed, show up to your appointments on time, and take your ideas seriously.

If you are having trouble managing when which contractors arrive, or other appointments with your real estate agent, it might be helpful to hire a project manager. They are able to plan meetings and appointments for you. It is darn near impossible to hold down a full-time job, a family, and a healthy social life, while conducting a house flip. You have more than just one house to maintain. If you're the type of person who likes to stay busy, it would be a wise idea to hire someone to organize all aspects of your house flip to avoid burnout and frazzled nerves.

While you are in the process of paying for repair services, it is important to keep every receipt. This will hold you accountable on how much you're spending on your repairs budget. If you make a checkbook and account for all things you've invested on the house, you will be able to see how much money you have left to spend on rehabbing. Furthermore, saving every receipt and holding yourself accountable for your spending will ensure easy filing when tax season rolls around. If you are organized in your finances, you will be successful in making a bigger profit from the flip.

One tip for rehabbing your flip is to give a little more attention to the front of the house, especially the doorstep. You could replace the front door. This is the first thing the buyer will see before entering the house. First impressions matter when it comes to selling your house. Tend to the exterior of the house as well as the interior to increase its aesthetic value and curb appeal, allowing it to shine inside and out!

4. Selling. So you found a house, financed it, and made fundamental repairs to it. With all of that hard work finally completed, it is now time to reap the fruits of your labor by, of course, selling it! Here is where you can become your own real estate agent—make the house marketable.

You can show off your flip by placing furniture in respective rooms, having fake plants, and even by having a bowl of chocolates on the counter. Practice furnishing the place. Make the house look as if someone currently lives there (without the communal mess, of course!) so that prospective buyers can imagine themselves living there. Get a real estate photographer to snap some professional pictures of your house, rather than utilizing pictures from your iPhone. A well-staged house can make the difference between $190,000 and $200,000.

Pay attention to the neighborhood of the house you're flipping. This is important to take into account because if there is a recent spike in criminal activity, it would make your chances of closing the deal seem less attractive. Nobody wants to live in an area where they're afraid their car will get broken into. If you see potential in a house with an increased crime rate, you might be interested in purchasing house insurance, which will protect your investment from any damages done by potential looters and squatters. You can also get a home security system, which will help add value to your flip.

If you notice a multitude of residents moving out of the area, don't lose hope. It could be that these are families with kids, military personnel, or businesspeople. Just lower the price or put work into the flip to boost its market value.

Most people think that a flip entails acquiring a foreclosure or a "carpenter's special," where it just needs a lot of handy-work to be done. However, during the real estate boom of the mid-2000s in the United States, investors would buy newly-built homes, hold onto them for a few months, and then resell them for a profit.

Pay attention to the timeframe during which you conduct your flip operation. It might suit your interests to buy a house during a recession, when homes are priced the lowest. Remember how more homes are foreclosed during economic downtimes, and the way banks want to scoop them up to maintain financial integrity. If you decide to buy now, residents may not be coming into the area right away, but the recession should buy you some time to work on your flip, increasing the value of the house. Once the economy exhibits recovery, your house will be ready to sell, and this could be a time of housing market prosperity.

For your first house flip, consider partnering with somebody more experienced. Look at whoever you're partnering with as a mentor or a house-market hero, not as a rival or an enemy. To those just getting into real estate, this person should be knowledgeable of the whole process. If they made some mistakes (and count on making your own, as well!) about house flipping, they could tell you what they might have done differently. Take this as a hip-pocket lesson and learn from others who are more experienced in the game of real estate. Normally, you can find these like-minded souls at home shows, on social media websites such as LinkedIn, or perhaps even among your coworkers!

You must build rapport with a team of people who will help you. Find an investor-friendly real estate agent who will find properties for you. As you browse your options, keep your budget in mind. Low-valued houses might be on the market for months, but it doesn't mean they won't sell. Older houses also depreciate as they get older, but with a little extra TLC, you can increase the value of the place with the help of an excellent handyman. You might put the majority of your investing into rehabbing the house to make it more profitable to buyers. And that's okay.

Furthermore, consider hiring a building inspector who can scrutinize every inch of your house. They can determine if it has safety issues, like termites, or a busted gas pipe that could turn your house into a gas chamber. It would be wise to get these problems resolved if you want your house to be made more habitable, especially in houses that have experienced heavy pet traffic resulting in lingering dander. Have the carpets replaced with either wood or tile floors.

You could be that one who is skilled in fixing up run-down houses, or perhaps someone who's skilled with a hammer and nails can do it for you. Invest in skilled craftsmen and your money will walk that much farther. After all, you wouldn't want a cheap architect to build a rickety stairwell just seconds from collapse, would you? You get what you pay for, so make sure that if your property needs renovation, you hire someone who will get the job done right.

For further review on who else can pitch in on your investment, review Chapter Two: "I Am The Recession-Investment-Automator!" Just know that you don't have to go it all alone. "House flips gone wrong" cause investors to lose money because they go in uninformed, if you will, on the tricks of the real estate trade.

When you finish your flip, you may not be able to recognise the house you originally bought (unless you decide not to renovate the place). Make sure to take pictures of the property, before and after, to get a view of your hard work. Snap some pictures during the repairs to track your progress. You might be interested in collecting these photos to put in a scrapbook to display as your claim to real estate fame.

So, as a summary, house flipping is a lengthy, challenging process to say the very least. I call it a process because there are steps you must take in a sequential order so that you can maximize the profits you earn from selling properties. I will list the steps you need to take to become a successful house flipping investor.

1. **Make your inventory.** First of all, you have to carefully consider what house you would want to turn for a profit, and where. Inspect the vicinities of your property first before grabbing the deed to the place. Analyze where you're personally at in your finances, and from there, speculate as to how much you're willing to invest in relation to how much you can spend in repairs and how much profit you can logically earn.

2. **Have some money.** You're an investor, so right off the bat, you should know that house flipping is an expensive but rewarding investment tactic. Most of us don't have the money up front to buy another house. Look into getting a home loan from the bank, or establishing a joint venture and share your profit with someone who will fund half of your project. But no matter which way you decide to finance your flip, make sure to budget everything. Round up when you estimate so you're not broke half way through, scrambling for cash.

3. **Start home improvement.** You start by contacting a building inspector, and having them scrutinize your house for safety problems, lest you want it to become a death trap for potential buyers. Have these issues fixed by hiring

contractors in the area, who can also repair other aspects of the house. Let these guys know specifically what you want done to the house in order to improve its value, and you can start watching your investment grow.

4. **Put it on the market.** Once you've replaced the carpets, installed the last cabinets and fixed the bathroom sink, you are able to sell your house! Give it that tidy-yet-lived-in look to appeal to the emotions of potential buyers; have them imagine what it would be like if they lived there. Pay attention to the front and back yards, as well as the doorstep. It's small things like these that could either make or break a deal. Either way, your goal is to sell this house as quick as possible, for the longer it's on the market, the more money you risk losing by keeping it there.

In order to more effectively flip houses and make more profit, there is much planning and forethought involved. If you know ahead of time the market you're heading into, you're that much more likely to succeed. Know the area in which you're selling. Know how to proportion your budget to avoid overages later on. But most of all, know yourself. Know your financial situation and know what you're capable of handling. If you find yourself too stressed out to take on the capacity a house flip provides, a few days off certainly won't hurt. Just know when to take a break and come back to the job in a timely manner.

Although you should know that house flipping shows on television don't portray the actual thing as it truly is, I encourage you to still watch them. Don't take them too seriously, but you might pick up some ideas on design tips or solutions to problems you encounter with the flip. Perhaps you greatly admire the way the cabinets were implemented in the kitchen, or they show an episode where the people experience a problem similar to yours. Relax and take notes on these shows every once in a while, and don't forget to go to the library to read up on some literature (such as this) about flipping houses.

The best advantage of house flipping is that you have the opportunity to network with others, seeking from them the help you need. House flipping allows you to meet many people, resulting in possible partnerships. Consider having to meet at least one person every step of the way. This, in turn, builds social skills, making you more personable. This gives the other party an advantage of having you as a connection. If done right, who knows, they could introduce you to some people who know some people, who want to conduct business with you. You never know who's willing to conduct a joint venture with you. Let them help you invest as you become more skilled in house flipping, and more people will win profits in the end.

Chapter Four

Rent-To-Own (RTO) for Profit

The housing market is accessible to all people, regardless of what situation they're in. Makes sense, right? It's not impossible in this day and age to find a place to live. Shelter is a basic human need. Taking that into consideration, landlords and property owners have ways of getting people in the door; they are reasonable enough to come to some sort of payment agreement with their tenants. Let's take a look at this example:

Carlton and his wife, Sharon, are expectant parents, and so they must move out of their apartment to make room for the baby. They determine that they want to buy a house. Carlton just started a new job that provides a stable income. Unfortunately, his credit history is shot, and Sharon needs to stay home to take care of the baby. This might put her career on hold for a few months, making Carlton the only source of income for the new family at the time.

As the investor who's trying to sell your house, you want to make this work for Carlton and Sharon, as well as sell your house for some profit. The couple states that they have the minimum required income to be able to keep up with a payment plan. They also express their desire to eventually own a house, but at the time, do not have the money up front for a down payment, and, with their credit, are unable to qualify for a mortgage. As the housing market is made to accommodate all people, how can you best serve the parents-to-be, Sharon and

Carlton? Your solution is to establish what's called a **rent-to-own** (RTO) plan, or a **lease** option.

You can benefit greatly from letting Carlton and Sharon rent-to-own. This kind of agreement lets the couple rent the house for a time period of 1–3 years, allowing them to save money for a down payment at the end of the lease. During this time, they make monthly payments, and this helps to repair and build Carlton's credit. The lease option allows time for Sharon to find a job, equating to a higher income for the couple combined. Their money goes directly to you. By doing rent-to-owns, investors get monthly cash flow with their down payment, and the agreed-upon price of the house by the end of the lease. This could be a very appetizing deal for you!

In this strategy, investors put their house on the market to find a tenant-buyer who has some cash that they have saved to purchase a home but can't seem to get qualified via traditional lending, as they have less than ideal credit or no credit at all. They may be people who have gone through a divorce, bankruptcy, foreclosure, credit payment issues or they may be people who have never had credit or are new to the country. They could be in the military with a family, needing a less-than-permanent option for a place to live, yet a practical solution to accommodate their dependents. These are ideal clients, as investors work with them to build qualifying credit over the next 1–3 years of the program that is called rent-to-own. This is different from a lease-option plan, which locks both the investor and tenant-buyer into the purchase of the home. What makes the lease-option so unique is that the tenant-buyer has the "option" to buy the house you're trying to sell. So you're wondering as to how you can get started. Read on and I'll start from step 1.

Let's say that you just flipped a house. You've had it on the market for several months, when all of a sudden your country begins to head into a recession. Suddenly, it appears as if nobody wants to buy houses anymore because their cash flow has decreased, along with the availability of work. With nobody able to scrounge up enough money to make a down payment, you offer your house as a rent-to-own. Now, more and more tenants show up at your open house showings, and it's up to you to narrow down the list and get a resident in as soon as possible.

Once you find an eager tenant-buyer who expresses their serious interest in your house, it's time to prequalify them. This is done as a process where, basically, you make sure they meet your needs and it's a reasonable enough deal for them. This can be done by ensuring their credit is adequate enough to at least get them in the door by ensuring that they'll make monthly payments, as well as possess the willingness to commit to a lease and an opportunity to purchase a home.

Once they are prequalified, they move on to meet with a licensed mortgage broker to see what kind of property they will be qualified for by the end of their lease, based upon the tenant-buyer's following of a set credit-rebuilding plan you two have established during the prequalification phase. When the mortgage broker has determined the amount the tenant-buyer is able to afford at the end of the lease option, they can now move on to meet their realtor to start looking for a home to purchase, which will most likely be yours.

When the tenant-buyer has decided that they're ready to move, they negotiate the purchase of the home with you, and sign the lease along with other contracts. What gets negotiated at this stage of the game is the price of the house, items on the lease, and the length of the term, which is typically 1–3 years.

Now, the tenant-buyer will make the initial option consideration payment that is typically 2–3% of the house price. Remember, this is the money that will go towards their down payment for the house; this doesn't get refunded to them should they forfeit the purchase. The reason is because this option is not a deposit; essentially, the tenant-buyer is investing in something of value, which is the option to be able to own the house.

After all payments have been made and documents are signed, the tenant can now move into the home whenever they're ready. On a continual basis, work with the tenants during the duration of this program, ensuring that they're on the track to successfully purchase the home at the end of the term. By the end of the day, it's beneficial for all involved!

Another approach to conducting this investment method is by way of the "tenant first" method. This strategy involves pre-screening the tenant-buyer and referring them to your mortgage broker and realtor to help them buy the house they want. The tenant is put in control of what they want, which is a house in an area that serves their needs. When the tenant-buyer is allowed to choose the home they like, they are more likely to become emotionally invested in the property and you're with them every step of the way. By having another person involved with your investment, you cut unnecessary stress and expenses out of what's supposed to be a positive money-making endeavor.

If you're getting hungry, you might take investing a step further and perform what's called a sandwich lease option. This method is perfect for investors who are just getting started or for those who do not have a lot of cash. A sandwich lease option allows you to buy a house by renting it for several years, exercising the option to purchase the property after accruing money put aside to cover the down payment. While renting the place from the owner (which is about to become you), you may sublease your property to other tenants. As they are occupying the house, they lease-option their house from you, who lease-options from the original owner. In a sense, the tenant-buyers are helping you make payments on the house you're letting them live in but, ultimately, you won't be the owner. Your tenants will be, and with the money they give you for buying the house, you can pay off the owner you originally bought the house from and, at the same time, make a considerable profit. Sandwich options are a great instrument of investment, because it allows you to invest without actual ownership. That's right, you never end up owning the home which you're making payments towards; the deed ends up in your tenant's hands after the deals on the house are closed.

In this method, you are both the lessee and the lessor, which means you rent the house from the owner, while also renting it out to another party. This puts you into many obligations. You must make sure that you're able to make payments on time in order to avoid defaulting on your payments and having the house foreclosed, which would automatically evict your tenants (not a good thing to bear on your conscience). Investing responsibility in your finances ensures monetary success, and a huge part of that is making sure your tenants are on the same page as you are. It's even better when everyone can make payments on time, so perhaps you can coordinate pay schedules to ensure peace of mind (for example, you may plan to pay the owner on the 31st, while your tenant plans to pay their rent on the 5th of every month).

The lease option is meant to be a hybrid between renting out and selling your investment acquisition. This means you get to be a landlord for 1–3 years. And a major part of being a landlord is knowing how to write a lease, the document that gets the tenant in the door. On this 1–3 year lease is an option at the end of the term that allows the tenant-buyer to purchase the home. If they don't wish to exercise that option, you still get to keep all the payments they made in monthly rent, and the money that was saved up for the down payment. Either way, during the time of the tenant-buyer's residence at your house, you cannot raise the price of the monthly payments, or rent/sell the house to anyone else. I know this seems obvious, but the lease in this scenario will not allow you to put the home on the market, not if there is a tenant-buyer who wishes to buy the place. Nevertheless, if you need help with the writing of the legal terms and conditions of a lease, simply find a sample online or consult your real estate attorney.

When you choose to RTO your house, you are gaining money all the time. This secures a more accessible profit only if the tenants can keep up with the payments. It's even better if they elect to follow through with the agreement to buy the house within a few years. Think about it. As I've previously said, you're getting a monthly cash flow from their rent payments. This will be happening for the next couple of years as stated in the lease. If the tenants follow through to buy the house at the end of the agreement, they will contribute a fee of about $2000–$5000, securing them into buying the house. This, along with the extra few hundred bucks they'll be paying in rent per month, will help offset the cost of the house or the down payment.

So, off the bat, you'll get more money by this method than to leave the house on the market, unoccupied. Then, when the tenants come around to buying your place, you're getting a huge influx of cash flow from the purchase. So, in all, this method tallies large profits very quickly for you, since you're getting cash flow from your tenants, and often. See what I mean?

You can easily put more money in your pocket by doing this easy real estate investing strategy. But you must know how to use good judgment in determining a house's worth. It's well-advised by the investing community to seek to buy a house that's priced below the market value.

For example, you find a condo that has been appraised at $250,000. However, the listed price is at $225,000. Bingo! You just saved a generous $25,000 (about the price to send a kid through a public four year university!).

Because the deed to the house is in your name, it's up to you (as the genius investor you are) to put on your thinking cap to try and raise the value to more than $250,000. This is a way you can put more money in your pocket. No matter what you do, you must convince the tenant-buyer to purchase the house for more than $250,000 (permitted it's done on ethical grounds). You could do some work to the house as you would a flip, but you don't have to do so as extensively. The ball is totally in your court for when you name a price. The amount of money you wish to harvest from this investment is entirely up to you.

Therefore, when you name a price, you should know how much the house will be worth in the 1–3 years the tenant-buyers will be occupying the place. Take the time to sit down and do the math. If you are able to agree to sell the tenant the house for $265,000, then you will make a net $40,000. This would be worth that new Porsche you've always wanted.

As every option to invest has its risks and benefits, let's go over the pros and cons of deciding to lease out your home.

As you've already heard, it makes a great amount of money. You're getting a substantial amount to rent out the place every month, and you're most likely going to sell it at the end of the three year period. But what if you can't find an eligible tenant to sign the lease. Carlton and Sharon, from earlier in the chapter, may fall below the eligibility line for approved credit. So, right off the bat, you might run into the chance that not all buyers interested in your place will qualify because of their credit score. This, in turn, could make the search for tenants a little more difficult.

A major factor in finding qualified tenants is where you find your house. You want the house to be located in a suburban area near grocery shops and schools, as this attracts a growing family like Carlton and Sharon from earlier in this chapter. It would be nice to find that perfect house that gets tenants in the door quick and easy. But if you cannot find one, even in your own price range (and trust me, there will be some cities where the housing market is so tremendous that it's just out of your ballpark completely), you'll have to center your investment approach on your tenant. It may give you less control over the deal you're making, but if you take the time to negotiate a sound, reasonable plan, you might end up making a generous profit after all.

Another disadvantage of the lease option is that when you do manage to sign tenants, you may run the risk of them not wanting to buy the house by the time the lease is up. This is okay, since the lease states that the option to buy is up to the tenant to decide. The upside of this is that you'll still get the monthly cash flow, plus the money that they saved for the down payment. Although you're getting less money than if they bought the house at the full price, it's better than getting no money at all. And, in a few years, the value of the home might go up, increasing your likelihood of garnering more interested tenant-buyers.

However, if the tenant-buyer does damage to the house that depreciates its value, you take the chance of losing money. Lease options require tenants to maintain adequate care over your property, but some tenants might have small kids or pets that, after moving out, compel you to replace the carpet or fix the windows. As a solution, plan on taking some time (we're talking like a few weeks) to rehab the house before it's ready to sell again, granted the tenant-buyers decide not to purchase the house.

With setting up your home as a lease option, you have to ensure that your assets are protected. For this reason, more legal paperwork is required to manage a lease option, such as background checks and contract writing. You may go to your local real estate office to request a background and credit screening application. These might require a fee, which the tenant-buyer can pay. You can also find out more about the tenant by contacting their employer and their last landlord, as well as one professional and personal reference. This process must be done during the prequalification phase, so you know ahead of time and receive the peace of mind that your property will be protected. You'll also get further information about their credit, and this is definitely important in knowing as to whether or not they will be able to make lease payments punctually. Don't forget to get to know your tenant-buyer. Take the time to interview them. Knowing what your tenant is going to be like before they move in can save you money and legal hassles.

Not only do lease options require commitment from the tenant-buyer, but they connect you to the area in which the house is located. You can go ahead and take a two-week vacation, but it won't be easy determining the logistics of moving elsewhere if something like work requires you to do so. If you don't see yourself in any given area for longer than five years, it would be a better idea to read on to learn of more ways to invest in real estate. There are ways to invest in real estate even if you don't count on living in any given area.

For the tenant-buyer, lease options are more expensive than original renting. Since lease options include a section that allows the tenants to buy the home, there is an additional fee they must pay; this goes toward a deposit which will offset the down payment if they decide to purchase the house. The price of the rent can be negotiated when it comes time to sign the lease. Normally, it would be wise to start suggesting rent prices at the fair market value of renting the property. This can be determined by a realtor who can appraise your house. Again, the increase in rent is about 20–25% of the price of rent. If you set the rent to $1200, then the tenant-buyer can expect to pay $100-$200 more per month, which, by the end of the term, will be forfeited if the tenant chooses not to follow through with buying the house. Therefore, out of the $1400 you plan to charge for rent in the given scenario, $200 will be credited towards the purchase of the house. Requiring them to forfeit this huge credit that gets built up over time (if they decide not to buy the house) gives them an incentive to buy the house, and the convenience to get out of the lease if they decide not to purchase the house or if they choose to relocate. Nothing's free, but everything comes with a choice!

And the choice in this scenario is the option to buy the house. If the tenant backs out of this clause on the addendum of the lease, you could sell the option to another party who will buy the house outright. Remember, options can either be exercised or sold. Once the tenants move off your property, it's pretty much fair game all over again. And, also recall that the longer the house sits on the market unoccupied, the more money you're losing since you must keep lowering the price to attract buyers. By acting quickly towards the end of the lease, you might find a tenant who moves in the day after the previous tenants move out!

Having an increased rent amount might cause the tenant-buyer to default on payments. If they fail to make payments, then they have breached a clause in their rental agreement that states they will pay rent each month. This is grounds to evict the tenant, which is a better idea than to let the house go to foreclosure. If the tenant fails to pay their rent, this means you would be losing out on money, making it harder to pay the lender for the house that these tenants are living in. If you don't see the money coming in each month, the house is likely to be foreclosed, putting a blemish on your record. By at least evicting the tenant, you're buying time to find new tenants.

Despite all the downsides of lease options, to RTO your house can be advantageous for all, especially during a recession. Economic troughs present hard times for financially disadvantaged families who experience unemployment, and, consequently, a reduced income and poor credit. You're providing these people with opportunities to improve their credit while building enough equity to offset the cost of a house during the eventual recovery of the economy (reference Chapter 1 for a review on the business cycle). Not only that, but because you'll be receiving money, you will most likely not be affected at all by the recession. It's a win-win situation, with the added satisfaction of keeping a family off the streets.

In analyzing whether lease options are the right way for you to invest, think about the time you have to invest on investing. Lease options are safer ways to guarantee your money's worth, since you get a monthly stipend from tenants. You also don't have to worry about maintenance, as the tenants are able to mow the lawn, change lightbulbs, and replace the fence for you. This may appeal to those who aren't knowledgeable on home improvement. Lease options allow you to automate your property by having residents occupy it, increasing your property value. Overall, lease options are growing in popularity since they generate greater cash flow than flipping houses, yet take up more time. Weigh your choices though, and determine if a combination of the two could be a better way to roll.

This is the first thing you want to do when considering a lease option: You must ask yourself, and all parties involved (like your spouse, if you've got one), if RTO is a sensible way to make real estate capital. Once you get past this stage, market, market, market! Place your house for sale and offer it as a rental, while scouting the area for tenants who want to own homes. The most eligible of tenant-buyers you can choose from might be those who *don't* have good credit!

When you've narrowed down your list of people you want living in your home, go ahead and initiate the pre-screening process. Remember, this process involves legal paperwork that might require help from your real estate attorney. Don't be afraid to get in touch with this right-hand man (or woman) for assistance with the legalities pertaining to background checks. A background check delves into the employment and residence history of an individual, as well as any significant criminal history which could make or break your deal. Being that you want to ensure your assets are protected to get the most value out of your money, your aim is to get a tenant-buyer with the cleanest background check and highest ability to make payments.

There are many pitfalls that can happen to lease options. For one instance, if your tenants cannot keep up with monthly payments, you risk losing your house to the bank due to foreclosure. To avoid having this happen, set an income limit. For you, this means to allow no tenants who make under your income limit, to reside on your property. Another mistake to make is by not writing everything down. Sometimes investors can get a bit forgetful. When you talk with your investment team and tenant-buyer party, one trick is to write down every number. You can later transfer these notes to legal paperwork, but it's never a good idea to agree upon what was said. It would behoove you, however, to keep track of everything on paper, so in that way you can at least backtrack and find your agreements recorded, signed, sealed, and delivered. You're to treat this deal as you would a sale. By this, I mean to be upfront and honest with your tenants. Act as the landlord and answer to any complaints they might have about the property. If your investment property has several safety discrepancies, get those taken care of in order to ensure that you're out of legal hot water, and that your tenants are happy at the house in which they live. Remember, you're the landlord, so meet with your real estate attorney to review the landlord-tenant law of your region.

The tenant-buyers take control of your property once the lease and other legal paperwork gets signed. They will need to pay the option fee, and remember that this money is not refunded to them. Some tenants tend to forget this attribute of lease options, and might try to sue you to get their money back. But like I said earlier in the chapter, this money is to help offset the down payment towards the house, and if the tenants wish to move out at the end of their lease, then convenience is ultimately the price they will have to pay. That's why it's extra important to have your tenant-buyers agree only to material that is written down. If you have to make them sit down and read the lease in its entirety in order for them to understand what they're getting into, this might save you legal troubles down the road. Either way, your mission is to allow your tenants to move in well-informed.

Once the prescreening process is done and you've finally selected one lucky tenant-buyer, it's time to draw up a lease. Leases include the rules (which you have set) for living on your property that are set in place until the tenant-buyer makes an official purchase and transfer of the deed. One tip is that when you write the lease, take into account all of the laws in your area. In the United States, the federal law requires that the landlord of any property constructed before 1979 must disclose the presence of lead-based paint. The law might be different in other countries, but I don't doubt that your real estate attorney would have the knowledge of current real estate law of your region. Include all disclosure requirements on your lease.

The lease option is one of many ways the housing market was made to accommodate a wide variety of people who are in different stages of their lives. Nevertheless, it is a practical way for many people to buy a house since it gives them the opportunity to try it out for a few years. As the investor, you will be able to negotiate your terms with theirs in order to make a winning compromise. This is one way you can help those who wish to live somewhere convenient for them. When you RTO your house, you can expect money coming to you each month, yet in smaller increments than if you were to receive money from selling a house you flipped. As well, you'll be handling home improvement issues far less often. Instead, you will get to handle people, not only building interpersonal skills, but more importantly, you aid in helping them with their dreams of one day having a house of their own.

Chapter Five

Agreement for Sales (AFS) are King

An Agreement-for-Sale or AFS, or House Purchasing contract, allows the seller and the investor in a property to conduct a real estate transaction by determining the contingencies that the buyer must meet in order to acquire what the seller is offering. It's 100% completely reliable and legal, and you don't need a real estate license to do it. *Please note that there are also wholesalers who find such properties as might interest an investor. They attain the contract, then sell it to the investor for a finder's fee, basically acting as a middle man between the seller and the investor who is looking to buy the property.*

The AFS process begins when you have found a homeowner who wants sell in a hurry for one reason or another — a situation that allows you to bid reasonably low on the property. This price will be the amount of money you will plan to pay the seller in a set amount of time, which is generally 1–5 years.

The key to making an AFS transaction is being able to offer a reasonable price on the house. Obviously, nobody likes being ripped off. When it comes time to negotiate a price, make sure it's sensible enough for the buyer to agree to, while ensuring that the price is right enough for you to make a profit. If you're a beginning investor, this might be a little tricky. Who decides the value of homes, and how is it determined? I mentioned earlier that you could get a home appraised. This entails hiring someone who is vested with the power to determine the value of the said home.

Get to know this person, the appraiser. They have been appointed with the authority to tell you what a home is worth. They scrutinize all aspects of the property. Obviously, the bigger and more elaborate it is, the more it's worth. Having land will add more value to the property, as well as having several other amenities such as a swimming pool or a verandah. It's also a plus if the home comes with a serviceable washer and dryer, as some properties have community washers that eat up pocket change. Hiring an appraiser to evaluate the worth of the home you are considering saves you time, and also helps you to avoid lowballing yourself or gouging the homeowner. Instead, you are playing fair.

So, when you have figured out the bidding price on the property, you are basically ready to meet with the homeowner to agree on a price at which the home will be purchased. This is the next step in figuring out how much profit from this house you're expected to make. Negotiating a price requires you to know what offer is fair and what is not.

***

As mentioned, AFS is a way to get into real estate investing without much cash and without a real estate license. It is also very low-risk when done right. But you shouldn't do it just anywhere. For example, if you are a wholesaler, it will work best where there are investors ready to take the properties from you. This generally means it works best in larger towns and cities.

The reason I'm talking about wholesaling is that it plays a significant part in AFS, as you are either a wholesaler who is buying cheap to sell for a profit to another investor, or you are an investor who is paying a fee to have ready-made deals brought to you. You just need to decide which of the two you want to be. There is a third option, of course, and that is being an investor who finds his or her own deals.

For example, suppose you find a homeowner who really wants to sell fast, and has a house worth $200,000. By the time you close, hold the property for some time, and sell, you might pay $5,000 in various costs. If you have brought in an investor (using an assignee clause in the AFS), he or she may want to use a real estate broker to sell, so those costs might total $10,000 or more. If you want to make $5,000 for your efforts, and the other investor wants to make $10,000, you would have to get the house for $175,000 (You arrive at that value by subtracting expenses from the list price: $200,000 - $5,000 -$10,000 - $10,000 = $175,000.).

There are two choices here: The first option usually involves you (as an investor) flipping a fixer-upper; the second option involves you (as a wholesaler) flipping the AFS.

Flipping the AFS vs Flipping the House

First, you look at the market, and then you do some research. Then you reach the decision that you can wholesale properties where you are. Perhaps you join the local real estate investor's club and get to know some people. In particular, you get the names and phone numbers of at least several investors who can make a decision quickly and who want to buy fixer-uppers. You should also make a note that it wouldn't hurt to check out what other investors are interested in, plus how much profit they expect to make on a project.

Now you go out to look for properties. Eventually, you find a motivated seller who is asking $190,000 for a house with problems. You compare it to others in the area and determine that it will be worth about $235,000 when it is cleaned and fixed up. It needs about $15,000 worth of work. Other costs, including a low-cost real estate broker, will run about $15,000, based on a holding time of about four months before it is sold and closed.

You want to make $5,000 for your time, and your most likely investor wants around $20,000 profit in a deal. Subtracting these and the costs, you arrive at a price of $180,000 ($235,000 - $15,000 - $15,000 - $5,000 - $20,000 = $180,000). This is the most you can offer. You start with an offer of $173,000, and eventually the seller agrees to $177,000.

In the contract, if you have decided to wholesale rather than invest, after your name as the buyer, you put the words "or assigns" or something similar (ask a real estate lawyer for the language that is used where you are). This little phrase gives you the right to assign the contract to another investor who will take your place and actually close the deal. You could also put in the contract a financing contingency with specific terms like: "This offer is subject to the buyer obtaining a fixed-rate 30-year mortgage loan at 5.0% annual interest or less." There are other ways to place a failsafe clause in the contract. Your best bet is to consult with your attorney as to how to write such a clause. With the proper clauses in the offer, all you risk is your time, and perhaps the good faith deposit or earnest money deposit you'll put down on the contract.

Now, let's turn the tables and say that you are the investor rather than the wholesaler. At this point in the deal, you would complete the repairs and retail the property. If all goes well, you might sell the renovated property for $240,000 and make a profit of $25,000. Good for you—the more you make, the more likely it is that you will use the wholesaler in the future. And don't forget, the wholesaler did all right as well. His $7,000 profit required very little investment or risk.

If you don't take the role of investor yourself, you need to remember a few things about wholesaling. Real estate is about speed as much as anything. You may have only a few days or a week to find an investor once you have a signed contract, and the investor needs a property that sells fast to avoid holding costs. To make this work, then, you'll want a list of investors ready before you start looking for properties. You should also focus on the houses that are selling fastest—probably those that are near the median price for the area.

However, if you set up the AFS without the middleman, and with the intent of investing in the property yourself, congratulations, you made a profit of $32,000 using a low-risk investment vehicle.

***

Investing Using an AFS

So, what if you would rather be the investor? What then? AFS' work great when buying homes that have little to no equity, and the owner needs out of the home.

Example: Client A bought a home last year and now they have lost their job or have to move to find new work. The home they bought was a three bed, two bath in Calgary for $420,000.00. They qualified for CMHC so they only put 5% down of the purchase price, equaling $21,000. They then got a mortgage on the remaining $399,000.00. Adding in mortgage insurance, the mortgage value is now $413,364.00.

Now, let's move forward one year later when they must sell, because they can't afford the payments anymore due to a job loss and are a few payments behind. They made their payments on the home for one year and have paid the mortgage down to

53

$401,307.00, but the real estate market in Calgary has dropped 7% and the home they bought a year ago is only worth $390,600. So, if we were to offer to buy this home for what's left on the mortgage of $401,307.00, we would lose $10,707.00 right off the top. Well, we couldn't call ourselves investors if we agreed to this deal. So, we get a bit more creative and we offer to do an agreement for sale on their home, and close on the deal in 3 years. But with this new offer, we offer to pay them $370,000.00 for the home. You might be thinking, "Wait a minute, Jason, are you crazy? They will never accept $370K when they owe $401,307.00 to the bank!!"

That's where this gets fun. If we do the agreement for sale, and close on this deal in 3 years from now, the mortgage will be paid down to $363,276.00, and we agreed to buy the home for $370K. That means the owner will actually make some money off this deal instead of losing money. If you recall, the market dropped, and the difference between what was left on their mortgage and what the house was worth at the time means the client would have to bring $10,707.00 to the closing table if they would have just sold the house on their own! It would have been even worse if they hired a realtor to sell the home as they would have had to pay his commission as well. So, you see, as an intelligent investor, we can create win-wins for everyone. The client sold their house that had negative equity (and made a profit doing it), and we bought a house below market value with no down payment, and we get to control the home for the 3 years. During the agreement for sale, we do have to pay the owner's mortgage payments, insurance and property taxes as part of most agreements. Of course, this can be negotiable like all things in a deal.

We don't do agreements for sale on homes for speculated appreciation of the market. That would make us speculators, and not investors. We only do these deals if we can control the property for the 1–5 years. If we can rent it out, and have a positive cash flow every month, or if we can renovate the property and flip it during the agreement period and rent it or sell it for a profit, then so much the better. Agreements for sale can create very large profit margins for our investing partners.

Let's use the last example, and, during the 3 years that we have the home under the AFS, we put a tenant buyer into the home for a Lease Option. Now let's look at how those numbers will pan out for this creative strategy. We agreed to buy the home at the end of the 3 year term for $370k, but its currently worth $390,600.00. So, going back to the Lease Option chapter, you will remember that we appreciate the home on average 3% per year for the term of the Lease Option; so, at the end of the term with the Tenant buyer, the purchase price they agree to buy it for will be $426,819.16. That will create a difference of $56,819.16 from what they will buy it for vs what we agreed to pay for the home. During the 3 year term, the Tenant Buyer is responsible for the maintenance and repairs (under $3k typically). You will also receive positive cash flow on this deal every month from the rent and the option consideration payment. All of this $56,819.16 was created without having to qualify for a mortgage or a down payment to buy the home. You will have to pay legal fees to draw up the contracts, so with the home purchase and the lease option contracts, you may have spent $2-5K. If it was $5,000 you spent, and you made $56,819.16, your return on this deal is approximately 345% per annum, and this being a 3 year deal, the return on your investment is approximately 1036% for this example.

Now, obviously not all returns are like this, but investing in real estate has created more millionaires than any other investment method in history, and thus the premise of this book is for me to help you become an armchair millionaire. How do we do this? We do it by asking you to invest with my team, and then sit back in your armchair as we make you a millionaire.

So, when you have figured out the asking price on your property, you are ready to meet with the potential buyer to agree on a price at which your home will be purchased. This is the next step in figuring out how much profit from this house you're expected to make. Negotiating a price requires you to know which offers sound fair, and which ones don't.

Chapter Six

Wholesaling in a Recession

Getting Started Wholesaling Real Estate

Getting started, a wholesaler should normally not ever buy a property. You put properties under contract with a contingency, and focus on quickly selling the property for more money to other investors. If you end up not being able to sell the property before you are expected to close, then you utilize your contingency and walk away from the contract.

A wholesaler is a middle man, and a good wholesaler becomes a very well paid middleman that other investors love. The thing is that if you have a good enough deal under contract, there are other more established investors out there who will be glad to pay cash for it in a matter of days. If you have a house that will sell fixed up for $100,000, it needs $10,000 in remodeling, and you have a contract on it for $55,000, then, with a developed investor network, you could have an investor buyer for it, for $60,000 in a matter of days. You sell it, or assign the contract for 60K— you bought it for 55K, so you just made $5,000.

Wholesaling real estate involves an investor buying a property, or getting a property under contract and then selling the house or assigning the contract as quickly as possible. The investor may wholesale the property to another investor who will then fix up the property and rent it or flip it. **The key to a**

successful wholesale deal is finding properties cheap enough that there is room for the end buyer to make a profit. It also pays huge dividends to have a stable of investors who know and trust you. It will take time to build such a group, but it is worth the expenditure of time and effort to make this happen.

Warning

You have to be very careful when you assign contracts on houses. Some provinces consider finding a buyer and seller to be performing the duties of a real estate agent. Even if you have the house under contract, it may be considered acting as a real estate agent if you assign that contract. If you are placing signs in the yard, advertising on Craigslist, or marketing with flyers without owning the house, it could be considered practicing real estate without a license. Check with your provincial laws before performing any of these activities!

How can you find properties to wholesale?

There are many ways to find cheap properties, but you must find very cheap properties to wholesale them. A wholesaler has to leave enough room for the investor to make a profit, and enough money for the end buyer to make a profit. Below, you will find many ways to find cheap properties.

Is it possible to wholesale properties from the MLS?

First of all, an MLS is a multiple listing service used by a group of real estate brokers. They band together to create an MLS that allows each of them to see one another's listings of properties for sale.

I do find properties on MLS, but it is difficult to wholesale them. Most investors keep an eye on MLS properties; the competition makes it tough for wholesalers to buy properties cheap enough. I think a wholesaler has to be able to act very quickly to get properties from the MLS, much like when I buy properties. It may be wise to get your real estate license and make a commission on these deals if you want to wholesale MLS properties.

Wholesaling off-market properties

I think a wholesaler's best opportunity is to find off-market properties. Off-market properties are not listed for sale, but the owners want to sell. The owners may be too far away, too busy, or too beat down to list the homes with a real estate agent. The owners still want to sell the home, they just need the right person to find them and make them an offer. Here are some great ways to find off-market properties:

- Attend REIA meetings: You may find investors or wholesalers with off-market properties at Real Estate Investors Association (REIA) meetings. Investors looking to get rid of homes at the meetings may provide a fantastic opportunity. You can also find buyers at REIA meetings, which is very important to a wholesaler.

- Send direct mailings: Send mailings to neighborhoods that you would like to buy homes in. The best way is with a simple black and yellow post card that says something like, "I would like to buy your home – Please contact me if you want to sell." Something simple like this will get the phone ringing.

- Advertising for off-market properties: Many investors advertise that they buy houses through the use of websites, bandit signs, and billboards. Marketing is never about just one approach. Try all of the ideas here. You'll never know which one will produce the property you are looking for.

- Websites: Some market to off-market sellers. The website sells leads to investors. I have never used these websites, but I know investors who have gotten deals from them.

It is not easy to become a successful wholesaler

The best tactics to get the best deals as a wholesaler are not easy to implement. It takes time and a lot of effort to buy homes off-market. If it were easy, all investors would use these tactics. But, if you are serious about real estate marketing and have very little money of your own, wholesaling may be your way in. Market to sellers in order to get the best deals to wholesale. When you get enough money to start buying properties to hold or flip, you can market to sellers to get the best deals for yourself as well.

How to get a contract on a house to wholesale

As a wholesaler, you have two options: Get under contract on a house, or buy the house and sell it right away. Many MLS listings require proof of funds or a pre-qualification letter — another reason it may be tough for wholesalers to buy off MLS. Also, if you are wholesaling because you do not have money to buy an investment property, it may be tough to buy a home to wholesale off MLS. If you are buying properties from off-market sellers, it will be easier to get a home under contract. The seller of an off-market property will not require a pre-qualification letter or proof of funds before signing a contract. Once you get a contract on the off-market property, you can assign the contract to another investor for a fee.

What does it mean to assign a contract?

Assigning a contract is a simple concept. The contract has a clause that allows it to be assigned, meaning that another person can step in and become the buyer without the seller's permission; and a wholesaler can actually sell the contract to another investor without buying the home. Anyone else can step in and be the buyer as long as they buy the home according to the terms of the contract.

How to use a double close to wholesale a house

It really is possible for wholesalers to buy a home and then sell it immediately without using their money. To do this, you need a great title company that will do a double close. The way it works is that the home owner sells the home to the wholesaler who immediately sells the home to the end buyer. The title company uses the end buyer's money to pay the original seller. Please check your provincial laws to make sure this strategy is legal in your area.

How does a wholesaler find buyers?

Once a wholesaler finds a house to sell or to assign, they must find a buyer! Usually the margins are very tight on wholesale deals and there is not room to pay real estate commissions. The wholesaler must find their own buyers in order to make the most money on their deals. A wholesaler must also close very quickly in order to assign the contract or complete a double close within the contract period. As I mentioned earlier, an REIA meeting is a great place to find investor buyers. Try to hang out where investors who buy houses hang out; trustee sales, auctions, and tax sales are all great places to find investors. Advertise to find buyers on Craigslist or in the newspaper. Finding buyers is an extremely important part of wholesaling and is often a wholesaler's biggest challenge. In some instances, one wholesaler will use another wholesaler who has more buyer contacts to help them sell houses.

Is wholesaling practicing real estate without a license

As a wholesaler, you must take the title to the home or sell your interest in the home. You cannot bring a buyer and seller together and take a commission or any other type of fee. This would be considered brokering a real estate deal, and you must have a license to do this. It is against the law to practice real estate without a license. It is also illegal in most provinces for a real estate agent to pay a referral fee to someone who does not have a license. You can send a lead to a real estate agent who then lists and sells the house, but you cannot be paid a percentage of the sale on that lead. There are some possibilities for being paid on a per lead basis.

How much money can you make wholesaling real estate?

Some wholesalers will never do a deal, and others do hundreds of deals a year. The money a wholesaler makes on each deal varies greatly depending on the wholesaler and the property. Some wholesalers make $2,000 on each deal, others $5,000, and some more than $10,000 on each deal. I know multiple wholesalers who are doing more than five wholesale deals a month, and averaging over $5,000 per deal. You can definitely make good money wholesaling, but, to do many deals, you have to spend money on marketing and have a great system. There will be many calls coming in from possible sellers, and you have to be able to talk to those sellers quickly, determine if the price is right, get the home under contract, and find a buyer.

Conclusion

It takes hard work and time to become a successful wholesaler. It is not a get rich quick business, but it can be a way to get started if you have no capital and really want to invest in real estate. I think the biggest benefit of learning to wholesale is that it teaches you how to find a great deal. If you can find great deals, there will always be buyers willing to invest in them. If you think you are finding great deals, but no one will buy them, maybe they are not so great. Knowing the value of a property and repairs needed is very important to being able to wholesale.

Chapter 7

RRSP Gold Mine

"Stop making your bank rich."

Saving for retirement can be difficult when you are only receiving 3% to 5% interest. Many investors are frustrated with poor returns and annual fees which they paid to receive, in return, non-performing RRSPs. If you're tired of the idea that your RRSP investments are only keeping up with inflation, this option might be for you.

RRSP Investments

Quite simply, RRSP investing is about holding real estate mortgages as investment vehicles under the umbrella of your RRSP account. This mortgage would be in place of stocks or mutual funds that by their very nature are extremely volatile investments.

Yes, RRSPs and Mortgages: they are a match made in heaven. Allow me to explain …

First of all, an "Arm's Length Mortgage" refers to a mortgage that is held within an individual's registered retirement investment account (RRSP). Many of you know that you can use your RRSP money with the Home Buyer's Plan to buy your first home. Many of you have done that already. Smart move!

Jason Meier

What the vast majority of you (and most real estate investors) don't know is that you can use your RRSP money (and other types of registered investment accounts) to invest in OTHER people's real estate. And when I say "the vast majority," I mean it! Most financial institutions can arrange Non-Arm's Length Mortgages, where you use your own RRSP money to fund your own, or a related family member's property. But there are only a few institutions in Canada that will allow you to fund someone else's real estate purchase.

Arm's Length Mortgages are very popular in Western Canada. With the help of these trustees—Olympia Trust, TD Waterhouse, Canadian Western Trust, B2B Trust—I plan to further educate investors on this little known, and highly successful investment gem.

To summarize for you, there are three different ways to use RRSP money to invest in real estate:

#1 Home Buyer's Plan

You borrow from your own RRSP to buy your first home (withdrawals must be repaid within 15 years).

#2 Non-Arm's Length Mortgage

You (as an investor looking to buy real estate property which is NOT your first home) borrow from your own RRSP, or that of a family member. The money is borrowed in the form of a 1st mortgage only (on residential or commercial property), is fully insured by CMHC, and you must qualify as with a normal mortgage. The mortgage repayment terms are not flexible and must follow typical bank industry standards.

#3 Arm's Length Mortgage (this is the one this chapter focuses on)

You invest your RRSP money into someone else's real estate. It can be in the form of a 1st, 2nd or 3rd mortgage, on residential, commercial, or industrial properties, as well as vacant land or recreational property. The big difference between this method and #2 is that the "someone" can NOT be related to you—as defined by section 251 of the Income Tax Act. In short, that means your spouse, family, or in-laws.

In a nutshell, you loan money out to a real estate investor who agrees to pay you interest on the money, and the real estate investor will pay back the loan at an agreed upon time down the road. As security for the loan, a mortgage is registered against the property so that your RRSP monies are protected.

You can use any registered product: RRSP, LIRA, RRIF, RESP, TFSA

An Arm's Length Mortgage is the MOST flexible way to use RRSP money. It is a sophisticated investor strategy that I plan on using for years to come for expanding my real estate portfolio and that of my investors.

While you can use any loan to value (LTV) percentage that you feel comfortable using, it is not suggested to go over 95% LTV.

Note: you can be in any position of mortgage.

1st position example ...

You have $95,000 in your registered account and you have a person that would like a mortgage on a property worth $100,000 at 95% LTV

The person would put in the 5% and you would put in the remaining 95%

You would use the appropriate documents to make sure that you are covered in case the person defaults on the mortgage

2nd position example ...

You have $20,000 in your registered account and you have a person that currently owns a house worth $100,000

They have a mortgage for 75% LTV on the property but they would like to pull out some equity from the property

You would get the appropriate documents in place and give them the $20,000 after you have placed a 2nd mortgage on the property

This would bring the LTV on the property to 95%.

If the person defaults on the mortgages, the 1st position mortgage would get rights to take whatever is owing on their mortgage first, then you would get whatever is owing on yours

The benefits:

- you get to choose your return
- your money is backed by real estate

- if you perform your due diligence there is minimal risk
- if you use your TFSA you will never pay taxes on the money you make

Now let me be clear: Investing your RRSP dollars in your mortgage is a fringe. Several financial institutions offer it, but not with much enthusiasm. It's costly and time consuming to set up, and it locks you into returns that could be lower than what a diversified investment portfolio could earn over the long term. If your entire RRSP is invested in your mortgage, then there's also a lack of diversification to worry about.

And yet, there's a steady level of interest in this strategy.

How to Do It

Investing your registered retirement savings plan in the mortgage on your home is not for everyone, but it can generate steady returns that beat what bonds and term deposits offer.

Step One

Find a bank, investment dealer, or trust company that offers this service; some investment advisers may also be able to help you set this up.

Step Two

Tally up fees – expect to pay a set-up fee, an annual mortgage administration fee, legal fees to set up the RRSP mortgage, mortgage insurance fees, and possibly discharge fees if you're breaking your current mortgage.

Step Three

Pick mortgage terms. Expect rules guiding the rate you can use, the mortgage terms available, and so forth.

Step Four

Use the money you're paying into your RRSP to diversify your RRSP investments, possibly by making regular purchases of stocks or equity funds and ETFs.

What You Should Know

Four things to keep in mind about investing your retirement savings in your mortgage:

1. You can invest RRIF money in your mortgage, but you must have enough cash on hand to fund the required minimum annual RRIF withdrawal.

2. Some banks will allow you to use RRSP money to buy a residential investment property, while others allow this only for an owner-occupied residence.

3. It may be possible to invest in a mortgage on someone else's property.

4. You'll need mortgage default insurance even though you're lending to yourself, and even if you have a lot of equity in your home.

Below are the several steps, documents, and timing required in order to set up an Arm's Length Mortgage. The fastest way to get your money working for you is to have your RRSP funds in a cash position in a self directed RRSP account that supports Arm's Length Mortgages (see #5 below).

1-Fill out an Investor Expression of Interest Form

This allows us to get to know a little more about you and what you are looking for in an investment.

Timing: 15 minutes

Form: Expression of Interest

2- We conduct a brief telephone interview

We like to get to know our potential investors, so we like to follow up with a brief call.

Timing: 15–20 minutes

3- We send you the Investment Package

4- Fill out an Investor Mortgage Commitment Letter

Timing: 15 minutes

Form: Mortgage Commitment

5- Sign up for a Self-Directed RRSP account

All RRSP mortgages must be held in a registered (RRSP, TFSA, RRIF, LIRA, etc) self-directed account by a trustee who supports Arm's Length Mortgages. You can set one up at one of these financial institutions:

- Olympia Trust
- Canadian Western Trust
- B2B Trust

Either of these institutions will work. Please note that it can take up to 3 days to get the account up and running.

Timing: 2–3 days

Form: RRSP Application

6- Liquidate existing investments to "cash"

If your RRSPs are invested in Mutual Funds, or another instrument like GICs, then you must liquidate them in "cash" form. This DOES NOT mean to withdraw them from the RRSP umbrella.

Timing: 1–2 weeks (depending on financial institution)

7- Transfer "cash" to the new Self-Directed RRSP account

Timing: 2–6 weeks

Forms: Transfer Form

8- Negotiate the terms of the mortgage

Timing: 1–2 days

Forms: ASP Canada Mortgage Worksheet

9- Get independent legal and accounting advice

We always recommend that you get independent legal advice on any type of investing.

10- Sign Arm's Length Mortgage Package

We will pre-populate the following documents and email them for you to sign and return. You can return signed documents via fax (or scan and email).

- Letter of Direction
- Arms Length Declaration
- Arms Length Mortgage Agreement

11- Submit all documents and register the mortgage

Our lawyer will submit all the required documents to the Trustee and register the mortgage. Once the mortgage is registered, you will get a copy of all the documentation for your records, including:

- Mortgage (verifies your security on the investment)
- Appraisal (verifies the Loan-To-Value)

12- You're Done!

You will receive quarterly payments and watch your investments grow in a consistent, predictable manner. As always, if you have any questions regarding your investment, we are only an email (or phone call) away.

Chapter 8

Recessions & Foreclosures

Recessions and Real Estate: It has been suggested that due to the economic impact of demographics, housing prices could be set for a significant decline in the next few years. As an example, a drop of 50% in the UK was forecasted, although this would depend on whether a global recession takes hold as expected in 2016. Such an event could be devastating; it could trigger a chain of events like the subprime mortgage collapse of 2008.

In many ways, the prospect of a global recession has loomed for over a year. The decline in oil prices could be considered as a precursor for this, as it underlined the weak performance of commodities and the impact that geo-political conflicts are continuing to have on the global economy. Then there is the fact that the Chinese economy has experienced a sustained and significant slump—one that is unlikely to be addressed any time soon. Even economies that have experienced growth in the last year (such as the UK and the U.S.) may struggle in 2016 as interest rates begin to rise in small increments.

This brings us to the property market, which remains a key driver of growth in the U.S. economy. The Federal Reserve in America is expected to confirm two incremental interest rate increases of .25% in 2016. This will increase the typical mortgage rate in the U.S. and force home-owners to pay more for their homes. We know that what happens in the U.S. is reflected in Canadian markets.

While this is not catastrophic in itself, the onset of another recession would change the financial and real estate landscape beyond all recognition. As interest rates rise, and property prices fall, existing home-owners will be forced to invest higher amounts while their investment weakens, leaving many burdened with negative equity, and mortgage agreements that they can no longer afford.

The circumstances may be different, but this state of affairs would almost certainly bring back harrowing memories of the 2008 recession. The impact would certainly be similar, with thousands of home-owners facing the prospect of either selling their properties quickly or simply foreclosing on their mortgage, and relinquishing their most valuable asset.

When the economy heads into a tailspin, you may hear news reports of dropping housing starts, increased jobless claims, and shrinking economic output. How does this affect us as investors? What does house building and shrinking output have to do with your portfolio? As you'll discover, these indicators are part of a larger picture which determines the strength of the economy and whether we are in a period of recession or expansion.

The Phases of the Business Cycle

In order to determine the current state of the economy, we first need to take a good look at the business cycle as a whole. Generally, the business cycle is made up of four different periods of activity extended over several years. These phases can differ substantially in duration, but are all closely intertwined in the overall economy.

Peak – At its peak, the economy is running at full steam. Employment is at or near maximum levels, gross domestic product (GDP) output is at its upper limit (implying that there is very little waste occurring) and income levels are increasing. In this period, prices tend to increase due to inflation; however, most businesses and investors are having an enjoyable and prosperous time.

Recession – Unfortunately, after experiencing a great deal of growth and success, both income and employment begin to decline. As our wages and the prices of goods in the economy are inflexible to change, they will most likely remain near the same level as in the peak period, unless the recession is prolonged. The result of these factors is negative growth in the economy.

Trough – Also sometimes referred to as a depression, depending upon the duration of the trough, this is the section of the business cycle when output and employment bottom out and remain in waiting for the next phase of the cycle to begin.

Expansion/Recovery – In a recovery, the economy is growing once again and moving away from the bottoms experienced at the trough. Employment, production and income all undergo a period of growth, and the overall economic climate is good.

Notice in the following diagram that the peak and trough are merely flat points on the business cycle at which there is no movement. They represent the maximum and minimum levels of economic strength. Recession and recovery are the areas of the business cycle that are more important to investors because they tell us the direction of the economy.

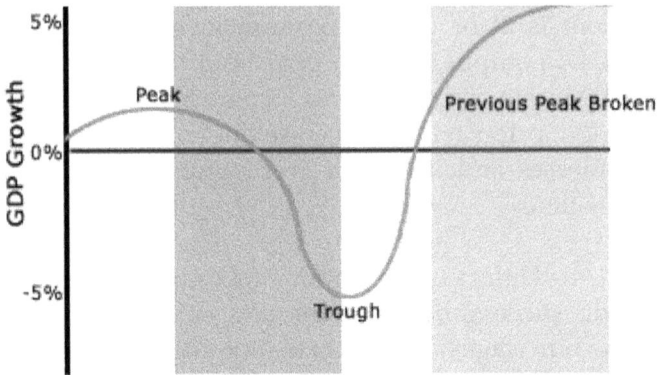

Recession Versus Expansion

Recession is loosely defined as two consecutive quarters of decline in GDP output. This definition can lead to situations where there are frequent switches between a recession and expansion, and, as such, many different variations of this principle have been used in the hope of creating a universal method for calculation.

The National Bureau of Economic Research (NBER) is an organization that is seen as having the final word in determining whether the United States is in recession. It has a more extensive definition of recession, which deems the following four main factors as the most important for determining the state of the economy:

1. Employment
2. Personal income
3. Sales volume in manufacturing and retail sectors
4. Industrial production

By looking at these four indicators, economists at the NBER hope to gauge the overall health of the market and decide whether the economy is in recession or expansion.

The tricky part about trying to determine the state of the economy is that most indicators are either lagging or coincidental, rather than leading. When an indicator is "lagging" it means that the indicator changes only after the fact. That is, a lagging indicator can confirm that an economy is in recession, but it doesn't help much in predicting what will happen in the future.

What Does this Mean for Investors?

Understanding the business cycle doesn't matter much unless it improves portfolio returns. What's an investor to do during recession? Unfortunately, there is no easy answer. It really depends on your situation and what type of investor you are.

First, remember that a bear market does not mean there are no ways to make money. Some investors take advantage of falling markets by short selling stocks. Essentially, an investor who sells short profits when a stock declines in value. The problem is that this technique has many unique pitfalls and should be used only by more experienced investors.

Another breed of investor uses recession much like a sale at the local department store. Referred to as value investing, this technique involves looking at a fallen stock not as a failure, but as a bargain waiting to be scooped up. Knowing that better times will eventually return in the economy, value investors use bear markets as buying sprees, picking up high-quality companies that are selling for cheap.

There is yet another type of investor who barely flinches during recession. A follower of the long-term, buy-and-hold strategy knows that short-term problems will barely be a blip on the chart when taking a 20–30 year horizon. This investor merely continues dollar-cost averaging in a bad market the same way as he or she would in a good one.

Of course, many of us don't have the luxury of a 20-year horizon. At the same time, many investors don't have the stomach for riskier techniques like short selling, or the time to analyze stocks like a value investor does. The key is to understand your situation and then pick a style that works for you. For example, if you are close to retirement, the long-term approach definitely is not for you. Instead of being at the mercy of the stock market, diversify into other assets such as bonds, the money market, real estate, etc.

Conclusion

The financial media often takes on a "sky is falling" mentality when it comes to recession. But the bottom line is that recession is a normal part of the business cycle. We can't say what the best course is for you—that's a personal decision. However, understanding both the business cycle and your individual investment style is key to surviving a recession.

Back to Real Estate ...

Foreclosure. One of the key indicators of economic downturns or recessions is an increase in foreclosures. Foreclosure in Canada typically does not make for a very good deal, because once a home has been taken back by the bank, the bank is required to sell the asset at fair market value. This means there are few good deals in Canada for foreclosure. As a result, in Canada, we do pre-foreclosures. This means we market and attract home owners who are going into foreclosure. The way this works is that once an owner falls behind in their payments, the home bank will send them out a letter as a notice to get their payments up to date. If they don't get the payments up to date, then the bank files the legal paperwork to proceed with foreclosure. From the time the first letter is sent out, to the time the bank is going to foreclose, is the time we want to talk to the client about purchasing their home!

This strategy is one where you are buying the properties at deep discounts because you are taking on other people's problems. The goal is not to be greedy but to ensure that the investors in the deal are making a healthy return for taking on the risks and problems of a foreclosure (as most people who can't afford their mortgage payments also can't afford to keep up with repairs). The strategy is the same for dealing with people in regard to divorce or inheritance, or with a distressed and tired landlord.

With the strategy I just described, there are many things you can do with the property once an agreement is made for the purchase. Here are some examples:

1. The "Buy and Hold" strategy
2. The "Flip"
3. The "Hybrid"
4. The "Joint Venture"
5. The "Rent to Own"

1. The Buy and Hold

The strategy for "Buy and Hold" is simple: buy a rental property that is under market value and hold it for the long term. The goal is to have the current owner (or new tenants) gradually pay off the mortgage so that in the end you have a property that is mortgage-free and on which rental income is being paid to you indefinitely. "Buy and Hold" is a popular option for Ontario investors, because it is one of the most straight-forward real estate investment strategies. As long as the property's income covers the expenses, and, as long as you have a minimum 20% down payment, it is also the easiest real estate investment to finance.

2. The Flip

In concept, the "Flip" is simple: buy a home significantly under market value, renovate it, stage it, and then sell it for a profit. As mentioned, however, it can take quite a while to find a great property to buy and flip. As well, it is typically easier to live through a "Flip" if you or someone you trust has home renovation skills. In any event, if done correctly, the rewards can be significant. On the financing side, it is a little trickier to obtain a mortgage for a "Flip" property since you won't be able to show an income from it until it is sold. Keep in mind that you may have to work with specialized lenders to obtain the necessary financing. The key to success? Ensure that you factor in all your financing costs when calculating the expected profit on your "Flip."

3. The Hybrid

The "Hybrid" strategy is a combination of the "Buy and Hold," and the "Flip." Most "Hybrid" strategies start with the purchase of a property that is undervalued due to the fact that it needs a fair amount of renovation or care, or is headed for foreclosure. The property is then improved with the intention of holding it for a longer term and renting it, or even leasing it, before ultimately selling when the market is favourable. As with the "Flip," you may need to look at financing the property more creatively, possibly using a combination of financing sources. Just like the "Flip" strategy, being realistic about your financing costs when calculating your expected profits is critical to ensuring that your investment goals are achieved.

4. The Joint Venture

Many investors who don't have (or don't want to tie up) funds in purchasing an investment property on their own, will team up in a partnership with someone with the same investment goals. In a "Joint Venture" it is vital to have absolutely everything in writing before any money changes hands. You should outline not only the initial financial expectations of each party but also things like:

- how you'll decide when or how to do repairs or renovations (and who pays for them)
- how you'll select tenants and who deals with them (if applicable)
- when you intend to sell, and based on what criteria

To obtain financing, make sure that your investment partner has good credit and is not overextended before sitting down with your mortgage professional to talk about your financing options.

5. The Rent to Own

The "Rent to Own" strategy has once again been gaining in popularity in Ontario. The way it works is investors purchase a property, but rather than advertising it as a traditional rental, they look to the current owner, or for future owners, who like the idea of leasing a home. These are typically people who want to own their own home, but can't, because they either have credit issues or an insufficient down payment. From an investor perspective, you would negotiate an agreement to have them purchase the property at a predetermined price, by a predetermined date. In addition, an "option fee" of a few thousand dollars is typically charged to secure the property. For a predetermined length of time (usually 2–4 years), market rent is charged, plus a predetermined amount is charged on top of the rent, which goes toward the tenant's future down payment. On the financing side of things, the investor needs to ensure that the property "cash flows" at the market rent. Just as importantly, the tenants or future owners should work with a qualified mortgage professional to develop and stick to a plan that will enable them to end up in a satisfactory financial position, with good credit, in order to qualify for a mortgage when the time comes for them to purchase the property

Chapter 9

Stocks Suck, *Especially* in a Recession!

Movements in the stock market can have a profound economic impact on the economy and everyday people. A collapse in share prices has the potential to cause widespread economic disruption. Such a collapse was responsible for the Great Depression of the 1930s. Yet, daily movements in the stock market can also have less impact on the economy than we might imagine. During the great recession of 2009–2013, the stock market performed quite strongly. This rise in share prices was rather misleading to the state of the economy. Also, a fall in share prices doesn't necessarily cause an economic downturn. There is a saying: *Stock markets have predicted nine out of the last five recessions! And its mistakes were beauties.* For example, the stock market crash of 1987 didn't cause any lasting economic damage—though it did influence monetary policy. For example, the UK cut interest rates in fear the stock market crash would cause a recession. Instead, low interest rates caused a boom.

Plummeting share prices can make headline news. But, how much should we worry when share prices fall? How does it impact on the average consumer? How does it affect the economy? And do stocks really suck?

Economic Effects of the Stock Market

1. The wealth effect

The first impact of falling stock prices is that people with shares will see a fall in their wealth. If the fall is significant, it will affect their financial outlook. If they are losing money on shares, they will be more hesitant to spend money; this can contribute to a fall in consumer spending. However, the effect should not be given too much importance. Often, people who buy shares are prepared to lose money; their spending patterns are usually independent of share prices, especially for short term losses. The wealth effect seems to be more prominent in the housing market, yet we know for a fact that value rises over time in real estate — at least it has always done so.

2. The effect on pensions

Anybody with a private pension or investment trust will be affected by the stock market, at least indirectly. Pension funds invest a significant part of their funds on the stock market. Therefore, if there is a serious fall in share prices, it reduces the value of pension funds. This means that future pension payouts will be lower. If share prices fall too much, pension funds can struggle to meet their promises. The important thing is the long term movements in the share prices. If share prices fall for a long time, then it will definitely affect pension funds and future payouts. People who hold enough real estate to produce the needed cash flow for retirement do not face such long-term declines, as rents tend to rise, and the properties are often being paid off by tenants. In terms of flipping, there are always bargains to be found, and sold, during a downturn of the economy.

3. Consumer confidence

Often share price movements are reflections of what is happening in the economy (e.g. a fear of a recession and global slowdown could cause share prices to fall). On the flip side, the stock market itself can affect consumer confidence. Bad headlines of falling share prices is another factor which discourages people from spending. On its own it may not have much effect, but combined with falling house prices, share prices can be a discouraging factor. However, there are times when the stock market can appear out of step with the rest of the economy. In the depth of a recession, share prices may rise as investors look forward to a recovery two years in the future. In other words: who knows what is going to happen with stocks? In real estate, time has proven, many times over, the staying power of property. Yes, prices may fall, but, over time, the value trend has always been upward.

4. Investment

Falling share prices can hamper firms' ability to raise finance on the stock market. Firms who are expanding, and wish to borrow, often do so by issuing more shares—it provides a low cost way of borrowing more money. However, with falling share prices, it becomes much more difficult. It may be more difficult to find investors during a stock plunge, but the real estate bargains that always show up in such times can usually draw out even the most reluctant of your money people. The one downside for owners can be a rise in interest rates.

5. Bond market

A fall in the stock market makes other investments more attractive. People may move out of shares and into government bonds or gold. These investments offer a better return in times of uncertainty, though, sometimes, the stock market could be falling over concerns in government bond markets (e.g. the Euro fiscal crisis). Times of uncertainty in the stock market are almost always good for the real estate investor with an eye for a bargain.

How does the stock market effect ordinary people?

Most people, who do not own shares, will be largely unaffected by short term movements in the stock market. However, ordinary workers are not completely unaffected by the stock market.

1. Pension funds. Many private pension funds will invest in the stock market. A substantial and prolonged fall in the stock market could lead to a fall in the value of their pension fund, and it could lead to lower pension payouts when they retire. Similarly, if the stock market does well, the value of pension funds could increase. Even if people don't own shares, it is quite likely people with a private pension will have some connection to the stock market.

2. Business investment. The stock market could be a source of business investment (e.g. firms offering new shares to finance investment). This could lead to more jobs and growth. The stock market can be a source of private finance when bank finance is limited. However, the stock market is not usually the first source of finance. Most investment is usually financed through bank loans rather than share options. The stock market only plays a limited role in determining investment and jobs.

3. Short-termism. It could be argued that workers and consumers can be adversely affected by the short-termism that the stock market encourages. Shareholders usually want bigger dividends. Therefore, firms listed on the stock market can feel under pressure to increase short-term profits. This can lead to cost-cutting which affects workers (e.g. zero contract hours), or the firm may be more tempted to engage in collusive practises which push up prices for consumers. It has been argued that UK firms are more prone to short-termism because the stock market plays a bigger role in financing firms. In Germany, firms are more likely to be financed by long-term loans from banks. Typically, banks are more interested in the long-term success of firms and are willing to encourage more investment, rather than short-term profit maximisation.[1] In my opinion, the volatility of the stock market makes it a poor investment, especially when compared to the real estate market. Why?

1. Real estate tends to go up over the long run. The same cannot be said for individual stocks.

2. Real estate does not require the diversity of investment that stocks do (as a mechanism for countering the volatility of individual stocks).

3. Stocks can suck for a long, long time. Thinking that you're mentally prepared for this type of environment is not enough. You must have a portfolio that truly matches your risk tolerance—not your risk tolerance today near all-time highs, but your actual risk tolerance. A properly constructed portfolio—one you can stick with through thick and thin—is what separates investors who can take advantage of cheap stocks versus those who get burned and never return.

[1] http://www.economicshelp.org/blog/221/stock-market/how-does-the-stock-market-effect-the-economy-2/

The S&P 500 has been essentially flat since the fall of 2014. Many newly-minted passives won't last much longer in their index positions, should the grind continue. And, if you throw in a disturbing drop, a la the 1973 example used at the link above, it'll go from a mild retreat out of stocks into a full-blown panic. People forget so easily. Just because it's cheap and easy to get exposure to stocks these days, that doesn't mean it'll be mentally cheap, and easy to stick with them.[2]

A recent article by *Business Insider* dove in to just how bad most people really are when it comes to investing.

First and foremost, one big problem is that investors often find themselves buying at highs and selling at lows, especially when volatility picks up and patience is tested. The problem is that so many people keep holding a stock for far too long, thinking it will turn around and move in the direction that they want it to. They then become emotionally invested in it and blind to the reasons that it WON'T move in their direction. If you follow our gurus' rules and limit your losses, you have less of an attachment to the stock and will be able to make better decisions. You still won't buy at the very lowest and sell at the very highest, but you buy lower than you sell, and still net a profit. Real estate sounds better and better, doesn't it?

"Amidst difficult financial times, emotional instincts often drive investors to take actions that make no rational sense but make perfect emotional sense," said BlackRock back in 2012. "Psychological factors such as fear often translate into poor timing of buys and sells."

[2] http://thereformedbroker.com/2016/05/05/qotd-stocks-can-suck/

Richard Bernstein, of Richard Bernstein Advisors, considers twenty years of historical data for this in a new research note. *"The performance of the typical investor over this time period is shockingly poor," wrote Bernstein. "The average investor has underperformed every category except Asian emerging market and Japanese equities. The average investor even underperformed cash (listed here as 3-month t-bills)! The average investor underperformed nearly every asset class. They could have improved performance by simply buying and holding any asset class other than Asian emerging market or Japanese equities. Thus, their underperformance suggests investors' timing of asset allocation decisions must have been particularly poor, i.e., investors consistently bought assets that were overvalued and sold assets that were undervalued."*

Bernstein's data is based on the buying and selling activity of mutual fund investors.

"They bought high and sold low," he added. *"When chaos occurred, investors ran away."*

Here's a chart that shows what Bernstein was talking about:

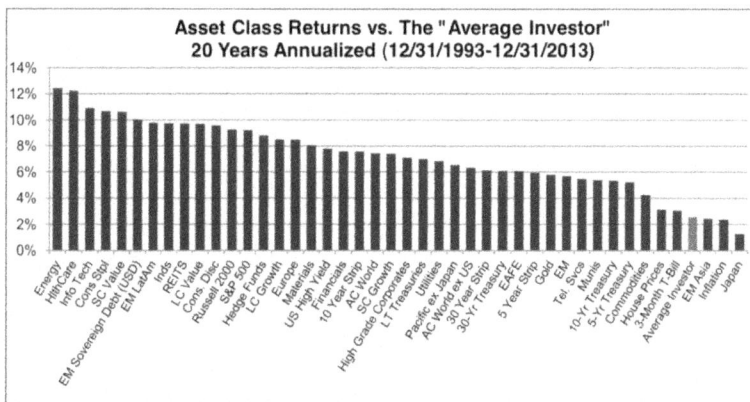

Asset Class Returns vs. The "Average Investor" 20 Years Annualized (12/31/1993-12/31/2013)

Source: Richard Bernstein Advisors LLC., Bloomberg, MSCI, Standard & Poor's, Russell, HFRI, BofA Merrill Lynch, Dalbar, FHFA, FRB, FTSE. Total Returns in USD.
Average Investor is represented by Dalbar's average asset allocation investor return, which utilizes the net of aggregate mutual fund sales, redemptions and exchanges each month as a measure of investor behavior.
For Index descriptors, see "Index Descriptions" at end of document.

Jason Meier

Some of our gurus get 100% of their trades right, but you'll hear them preach over and over again that the driver of their success is limiting losses. The famous economist John Maynard Keynes once said "Markets can remain irrational longer than you can remain solvent." It basically means that your investment thesis could be completely right, but the market may not realize that until you've been forced out of your position due to massive losses. I don't think any of us could have said it better ourselves.

Let's take a look at average real estate prices over a similar period:

NEW HOME PRICES IN CANADA

AVERAGE PRICE FOR ABSORBED UNITS, SINGLE & SEMI-DETACHED IN METRO AREAS WITH AT LEAST 50,000 RESIDENTS

IN THOUSANDS OF DOLLARS

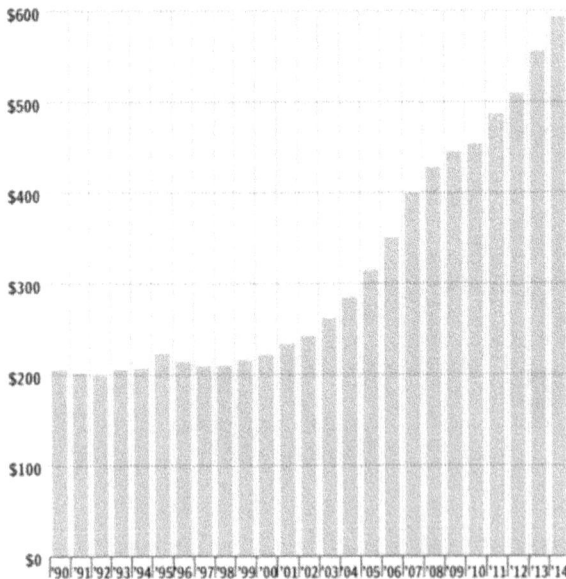

SOURCE: CMHC MARKETS ABSORPTION SURVEY

NATIONAL POST

Chapter 10

Finding the Deals

As this was mentioned in a previous chapter, you should realize that you make your profit when you buy. To make this profit, **you must purchase a property at a price that ensures you make your desired profits based upon your ability to execute your exit strategy.** In other words, you need to buy smart. If you overpay for a property, no amount of wishing, hoping, or improvement is going to make your investment worthwhile. How do you find that kind of deal? Here's one example:

610 Park Street is currently listed at $145,000, and recent sales show that similar homes in that neighbourhood have sold for between $140,000 and $170,000. The house, however, needs about $25,000 worth of work to be in nice condition. Therefore, if you pay $145,000 for it and put in $25,000, you'll be at $170,000, and that doesn't count all the closing costs, holding costs, selling costs, unforeseen overages, or other fees that you'll have to pay. You'll owe more than the property is worth—no matter how much work you do to it. However, if similar homes were valued at $225,000, you would find that you had indeed made your profit when you bought. The same principle applies to rental investment properties.

It's often said by experienced investors that appreciation is the "icing on the cake." In other words, don't count on the market swinging upward. You make your profit when you purchase a property based on what it would be worth today, not what it might be worth someday. If an investment makes no sense without appreciation, don't "speculate." Walk away; don't invest. Speculation is a dangerous business, even for seasoned investors.

Now that you understand the importance of locking in your profit at purchase, it's time to start looking for a property. First, however, **you need to define your selection criteria.** This section will focus on what your criteria is, why it matters, and how to define it.

Your selection criteria list is just like a shopping list. It's designed to keep you focused on shopping for the things you need and not waste money on other good looking things along the way. Real estate is an exciting field with a lot of different niches and strategies, so it is easy to get distracted by the next big thing or trend. Having clearly defined selection criteria can help you stay focused, avoid becoming overwhelmed, and keep you on track to buy a great investment property. By defining your criteria, you'll be able to narrow down the choices in the market, and you'll then eliminate the vast majority of deals that are only distractions. Instead, you'll focus on finding just the kind of deals that you are interested in buying.

Creating Your Selection Criteria

It's now time to choose your niche and strategy and come up with a list of criteria to narrow down your selection further. There are a number of different items you will want to consider to add to your "criteria list." These *could* include:

- **Town**
  What are the long term benefits of investing in this town? Is it poised for growth, or is the market stagnant? Is it a buyer's

or seller's market? Do these answers support your exit strategy?

- **Neighborhood**
  What have other homes in the neighbourhood sold for? Are these homes equivalent to the one you're interested in? If the house is decked out beyond the average home in the neighbourhood, does the seller expect to sell at a higher than average price?

- **Property Size (Square Feet)**
  The number of square feet in a home or rental unit is something that is a defining parameter used by almost all buyers and sellers. Make sure that you have been given the correct square footage before proceeding with any deal. Decide what size of buildings you are interested in purchasing.

- **Lot Size**
  Is the property a "full lot?" Is there more land being offered than might be expected? The more land being offered, the higher the value. What size of property are you looking for?

- **Property Conditions**
  One must understand that it is land that appreciates, and the home that depreciates. What developments have been made to the property? How does this compare to others in the neighbourhood? Are you willing to purchase anything less than a fully developed property?

- **Number of Units**
  Are you buying a condo or a multi-family dwelling? You need to decide how many units you want to be responsible for. A four-unit dwelling, or a single condo unit, is ideal for someone just starting in real estate investing.

- **Cap Rate**

  The capitalization rate is the rate of return on a real estate investment property based on the income that the property is expected to generate. The capitalization rate is used to estimate the investor's potential return on his or her investment—**Capitalization Rate (Cap Rate) = Net Operating Income (NOI) / Current Market Value.** So, for example, if a property was listed for $1,000,000 and generated an NOI of $100,000, then the cap rate would be $100,000/$1,000,000, or 10%.

- **Cash Flow**

  The value of any cash-flow producing asset is the present value of the expected cash flows on it. Just as discounted cash flow valuation models, such as the dividend discount model, can be used to value financial assets, they can also be used to value cash flow producing real estate investments. To use discounted cash flow valuation to value real estate investments, it is necessary to measure the riskiness of real estate investments and to estimate a discount rate based on the riskiness. It is also necessary to estimate expected cash flows on the real estate investment for the life of the asset.

  Discounted cash flow analysis, or DCF, is very commonly used in evaluation of real estate investments, although determining the discount rate involves a number of variables that may be difficult to predict accurately. Discounted cash flow analysis is a valuation method that seeks to determine the profitability, or mere viability, of an investment by examining projected future income or cash flow from the investment, and then discounting that cash flow to arrive at an estimated current value of the investment. This estimated current value is commonly referred to as net present value, or NPV. For evaluation of real estate investments, the discount rate is commonly the desired or expected annual rate of return.

For real estate investments, the following factors need to be included in the calculation:

Initial cost – Either the purchase price or down payment made on the property.

Financing costs – The interest rate costs on any initial or expected financing.

Holding period – For real estate investments, the holding period is generally calculated for a period of between five and 15 years, although it varies between investors and specific investments.

Additional year-by-year costs – These include projected maintenance and repair costs, property taxes, and any other costs besides financing costs.

Projected cash flows – A year-by-year projection of any rental income received from owning the property.

Sale profit – The projected amount of profit the owner expects to realize upon sale of the property at the end of the projected holding period.

A number of variables must be estimated in the DCF calculation; these can be difficult to pin down precisely, and include things such as repair and maintenance costs, projected rental increases and property value increases. These items are usually estimated using a survey of similar properties in the area. While determining accurate figures for projecting future costs and cash flows can be challenging, once these projections and the discount rate are determined, the calculation of net present value is fairly simple and computerized calculations are freely available.

Appreciation Potential

Some things to consider when trying to assess the potential appreciation of the property that you are considering to purchase:

1. **Employment Opportunities:** Locations with a growing job market tend to attract more people. More people means more renters or buyers, especially if you target an area with a large rent/own ratio. You can visit Statistics Canada for reliable and timely data on the labour market for the area you are considering. If you notice a large corporation moving to the area, migration will follow. College towns are now also a viable option as there is the steady flow of students needing off-campus housing, although the demand may only be strong for the September to April school year.

2. **Location, Location, Location:** The quality of the location will influence the type of renters or buyers attracted to your property. Look at criteria, such as proximity to transportation, hospitals, universities and colleges, major business centres, local restaurants, and shopping. The more central the location, the greater the demand.

3. **Rent:** For income properties, your monthly rent is your staple. Find out what the average rental rates are in the area. Can you achieve above or below the average? At the very least, you are going to want to cover your mortgage payment, taxes, and miscellaneous expenses like insurance. If this can be achieved, then you can move on.

4. **Safety:** No one wants to live in an unsafe neighbourhood. You can inquire about crime rates. Again, Statistics Canada is a great resource, and even the local police department can tell you whether the neighbourhood is safe and secure.

5. Amenities: What attractions are nearby that will be both a draw and a requirement for renters or buyers? Things that must be considered are shopping malls, parks, movie theatres, gyms, and access to public transportation.

6. **Schools:** One of the top considerations for your renters/buyers may hinge on the school district, and specific schools that they want their children to attend. Researching the local schools will be appreciation of your investment property.

7. **Future Development:** What developments are planned for the area which would positively or negatively impact the value of your property? Is it a high-growth area, or one that is currently in decline? A neighbourhood in the early stages of gentrification might result in a faster and higher appreciation for your investment property.

8. **Inventory:** Is there a lot of inventory available on the market? Make sure you look at market trends for the last few years, as you don't want to be in a seasonal trend only when making your investment decision. For rental units, you have to review the vacancy rates that have existed based on inventory levels and how this may impact your monthly rental rates. The same goes for investment properties; are you in a seller's market, or are units moving more slowly?

9. **Property Taxes:** These costs affect your bottom line. Review the taxes and the current market value assessments and determine if they are high and, if so, whether there's a reason.

10. **Insurance:** These are additional costs that erode your bottom line returns. Of course, you don't want to invest in areas where you cannot get insurance, like flood plains or possible

proximity to natural disasters. You can do your research with your insurance agent to determine the risks of claims that might exist, and if you can get coverage at all.

The easiest, and possibly the best, investment properties for beginners are residential single family homes and condominiums. Condos are low maintenance, as generally the condo corporation is responsible for external repairs. You must keep an eye out for high maintenance fees which are generally charged on a cost per square foot, per month basis. Do your research and comparative analysis to ensure these costs are in line for the building in question.

When you have the type of property you desire and the neighbourhood narrowed down, look for the best properties that have both appreciation potential and good projected cash flow. You should choose an experienced and seasoned realtor who has a proven track record of helping buyers with the acquisition of investment properties. You'll want a successful realtor to help and advise you with this exciting opportunity!

No one can tell you exactly what your investment property criteria should or should not include. Some of it will come down to personal preference such as, "I only want to buy in Seattle," or "I only want houses with basements," but most of your chosen criteria will revolve around the kind of investment you are getting into. For example, if you are looking to become a "buy and hold" investor of small multifamily units, your criteria's going to include small multifamily properties, and will exclude old commercial buildings.

By specifying ahead of time what criteria you are willing to look at, your search becomes much more manageable. In the same way, you are able to more effectively communicate your desires to others who may help you buy property. If you simply told people, "I'm looking for real estate," the most likely response would be, "Good for you ...." However, if you instead mentioned that you were looking to buy a small single family house in the Rockford neighborhood for under $150,000, you enable others to think of properties that might match that description and get you connected with the deal.

Perhaps the most important part of the criteria you put together is the financial component. If a deal doesn't make sense financially, it's not going to be a strong investment for you. We have looked at some of the basic math surrounding real estate investing, such as income, cash flow, and return on investment. However, generally speaking, a listing is not going to tell you the important information you want to know about the financials of a property. Yes, you can generally determine the amount of income the property makes, but you won't know immediately how much monthly cash flow the property produces, how overpriced the property is, or what you should offer. Additionally, it's not going to make sense to get out your spreadsheet and do a full property evaluation on every single deal you glance at. This is when "rules" come into play.

A "rule" is short for "rule of thumb." Rules can help give you a quick way to evaluate a property's financials *on the fly*. As with any "rule of thumb," using rules is not an exact science and should never be relied on entirely to decide if a property is a good investment. However, they can help you quickly filter a property and decide if it's worth further evaluation. Let's take a look at a few of these rules:

The 2% rule states that your monthly rent should be approximately 2% of the purchase price. In other words, a $100,000 home should rent for $2,000 per month; a $50,000 home should rent for $1,000 per month. This is a very conservative estimate that is very simplistic, but can help in deciding if a property warrants a deeper look. In most parts of the country, the 2% is very difficult to achieve, but the closer you can get to 'that, the better cash flow you'll receive.

Real World Example: An average three-bedroom home rents for $800 per month in your neighborhood. According to the 2% rule, you should be looking to spend around $40,000 for that property ($800 / .02 = $40,000).

The 50% rule is a great rule-of-thumb that helps you to fairly accurately predict how much your expenses are going to cost you each month for a property. The 50% rule simply states that 50% of your income will be spent on expenses—including the mortgage payment. As mentioned above, most real estate listings will let you know what the monthly income of a property is. By dividing that number in half, you are able to easily see how much you'll have left to pay the monthly mortgage (principal and interest). Any income left over, after the 50% of expenses and the mortgage payment are taken out, is your cash flow. The 50% of expenses includes all expenses, including repairs, vacancies, utilities, taxes, insurance, management, turnover costs, and the occasional "big ticket" repairs that must be saved up for (aka Capex or Capital Expenses, like roofs, parking lots, furnaces).

Real World Example: An apartment building brings in $8,000 per month in income. Using the 50% rule, we are left with $4,000 to make the mortgage payment. If the monthly mortgage payment on the property was $3,500 per month, you can reasonably assume a monthly cash flow of $500 per month.

The 50% rule is especially helpful in teaching that expenses are almost always more than one might think. One common mistake that new investors make is underestimating how much the expenses are going to cost. The 50% rule helps to show that there are always costs that are unexpected, so plan for them.

The 70% rule is used by investors to quickly determine the maximum price one should pay for a property based on the after repair value (ARV). Though most often used by house flippers, the 70% rule can actually be used for any strategy when you want to find a good deal. The 70% rule says that you should only pay 70% of what the after repair value is, less the repair costs.

Real World Example: A home which, after being fixed up, should sell for approximately $200,000, needs approximately $35,000 worth of work. Using the 70% rule, a person should multiply $200,000 by 70% to get $140,000,and then subtract the $35,000 in repairs. The most a person should pay for this property, therefore, should be $105,000.

Remember, a rule of thumb, like the ones above, is used only to quickly and efficiently screen a property and decide if it's worth further investigation. Never use a "rule of thumb" to decide exactly how much to pay, or if you should invest or not. If a property passes the above rules (or gets close), it may be worth a more detailed analysis on paper or via a computer spreadsheet. Don't confuse a rule of thumb for a license to skip doing your homework.

Where to Find Real Estate Investments

When you have your criteria set, it's time to start looking for your investment property. No doubt you've seen "For Sale" signs in front of homes, but there are many other ways to find investment properties. This section will explore various different ways that you can use to find properties—the list is not exhaustive, but a good start for any new investor.

The MLS

The MLS, short for the Multiple Listing Service, is a collection of properties for sale by different real estate brokers across the country. When you search a site like Realtor.com or Redfin.com, you are actually searching the MLS. This information is widely distributed for the most eyes to see.

The Newspaper

While quickly fading from use, the classified section of your local newspaper is a good place to look for homes that are "For Sale by Owner." Oftentimes, real estate agents will also put their listings in the newspaper, so it can be a bit challenging to determine what is listed on the MLS and what is not. You can also place your own ads in the newspaper.

Word of Mouth

Some homes are simply sold the old fashion way—by word of mouth. By letting everyone know that you are in the market to buy (and defining your criteria, as discussed above), you place yourself in the best position to find deals via word of mouth. You can do this directly with peers, at your local real estate club, or in the BiggerPockets Marketplace.

Craigslist

Craigslist.org is a free online classifieds website that is currently the #51 most popular website in the world. Millions of people use Craigslist.org to buy, sell, trade, or give away almost anything you can imagine—including real estate.

Outbound Marketing

Outbound marketing is when you go out and bring sellers to you. This can involve advertising, direct mail, or a number of other marketing techniques. The problem to consider with marketing is that it costs money—money that must be added to your bottom line when you do make a purchase.

Loopnet.com

Loopnet.com is the web's largest marketplace for commercial properties. From small multifamily properties, to apartment complexes, shopping malls, fast food restaurants, and more, Loopnet.com is the place to search for publicly listed commercial properties for sale.

Yard signs

An easy and cost effective way to get your message out there—in the specific neighbourhoods you wish to target. Beware of bylaw enforcement rules.

Postcards

These can be mass delivered in your target market, mailed to a specific list of prospects or even dropped in the mailbox of a property you're interested in. It is an opportunity for a follow-up where you begin a conversation. Again, the cost of doing this adds to your bottom line when you make your purchase.

Driving for dollars

This is when you go driving around looking for deals in areas that need repairs, and leave a note on the door or in the mailbox stating that you want to buy the home. You can also knock on the door and talk to the owner, or, if a rental, ask for the owner's info.

Go walking around the neighborhood

Ask people if they know anyone who is planning to move and wants to sell their home. You never know what opportunities you will discover, or even create.

Billboard signs

Only for major players as this is very expensive.

Call other wholesalers

See if they have deals they are trying to move.

Social Media

Facebook Pages, Twitter, etc. These are great venues as they only cost you the time you put into them.

Websites

Create multiple websites to drive traffic. WordPress is a great platform as it's easy to learn, easy to use and is completely free. You will have to buy the Domain names you want to use and either set up a server or buy bandwidth from someone else.

Blogs

Write an article about what you do and have someone post it on a blog, or, better still, start a blog of your own. Linked-in or Facebook provide free platforms on which to build your blog.

SEO (Search Engine Operation)

This is incredible for websites and blogs, and is a must if you want leads. You can hire SEO companies to submit your URL, etc. to thousands of search engines for a nominal fee.

Talking with other investors and REI Clubs

See what people are working on and see if what they are doing is something you can help them with. Be open to joint ventures.

Business cards

Pass them out. They don't do any good in your pocket.

Call rental signs

See if the landlord is fed up and would rather sell.

Call properties that have been on the MLS for 90 days plus

See if they are willing to move on their pricing.

Call FSBO (For sale by owners)

See how low they will go.

Flyers

Post them in local stores and bulletin boards. With today's desktop publishing options, and companies like VistaPrint, it is easy and affordable to create your own flyers.

Vehicle advertising

Do decals, or a vinyl wrap that says "We buy houses."

Bird Dogs

People you give a finder's fee to if they can bring you the type of deals you are looking for.

Mortgage brokers

These are a great way to find rent-to-own clients. It's a good idea to have mortgage brokers as part of your team. They can be as important as lawyers and your banker.

Realtors

A great place to get leads for properties that aren't very nice looking and have potential value.

Divorce lawyers

They can pass your info to clients needing to sell quickly.

City bylaw enforcers

They will have info on properties that are eye sores, or even just vacant.

Basically, everyone is a lead generating machine if you can explain to them what's in it for them.

So, there you have it: a detailed program for finding, fixing, selling, or holding onto real estate—in a profit oriented fashion. Soon, you too, will be on your way to becoming an Armchair Millionaire.

Jason Meier

NOTES

NOTES

NOTES

NOTES

NOTES